SO-CAA-036

93
106

Shooting Star

PUTTING **HEART** INTO HOME CARE

JIM FLICKINGER

Shooting Star

PUTTING

HEART

INTO

HOME CARE

Copyright © 2020 by Jim Flickinger.

All rights reserved. No part of this book may be used or reproduced in any manner whatsoever without prior written consent of the author, except as provided by the United States of America copyright law.

Published by Advantage, Charleston, South Carolina.
Member of Advantage Media Group.

ADVANTAGE is a registered trademark, and the Advantage colophon is a trademark of Advantage Media Group, Inc.

Printed in the United States of America.

10 9 8 7 6 5 4 3 2 1

ISBN: 978-1-64225-160-9
LCCN: 2011000000

Book design by Matthew Morse.

This publication is designed to provide accurate and authoritative information in regard to the subject matter covered. It is sold with the understanding that the publisher is not engaged in rendering legal, accounting, or other professional services. If legal advice or other expert assistance is required, the services of a competent professional person should be sought.

 Advantage Media Group is proud to be a part of the Tree Neutral® program. Tree Neutral offsets the number of trees consumed in the production and printing of this book by taking proactive steps such as planting trees in direct proportion to the number of trees used to print books. To learn more about Tree Neutral, please visit **www.treeneutral.com**.

Advantage Media Group is a publisher of business, self-improvement, and professional development books and online learning. We help entrepreneurs, business leaders, and professionals share their Stories, Passion, and Knowledge to help others Learn & Grow. Do you have a manuscript or book idea that you would like us to consider for publishing? Please visit **advantagefamily.com** or call **1.866.775.1696**.

This book is dedicated to our beloved patient families who, in humility, come to us with personal needs we can fulfill most of the time. They have helped make BrightStar Care of Central DuPage–Wheaton the exceptional organization it is today.

Contents

Foreword

"Nice opportunity" was the first thought that came to my mind when Jim Flickinger asked me to pen this foreword. It meant that I would be able to join with Jim, albeit in a very small way, on a project of his that I know will be helpful to many folks at a time when they most need it. In short, Jim's book—like so many of his steps taken in developing a business that does so much for the community—is a perfect example of the business motto that my own business partner and I adopted when we founded our company nearly twenty years ago: "Do the right thing at the right time." I also chuckled at myself. Why? Because that first thought is one that is quintessentially characteristic of Jim himself. He embraces opportunities—so long as they also involve being nice in some way.

My older sister Jennie and I came to know Jim rather closely across the past decade. I'm able to speak for both of us when saying that this period surely ranks among the best times of our lives. This is because of what Jim and his wife, Judy, along with their team members, did to make our beloved father's final years very happy and comfortable under their utterly outstanding home care. The value of what Jim and his company provided for Dad—and for all of my siblings and the rest of our family—was highlighted by the stark contrast between those superb services and the utterly frustrating and miserable time we previously experienced when obtaining home health care for our mother, who declined and died long before Jim founded his company. For good reason, Jennie and I quickly developed considerable affection for Jim and Judy. More important for purposes of this foreword, my admiration for Jim's acute acumen and well-tempered wisdom is every bit as strong as the respect I developed for the most talented of the many business leaders whom I met and worked with during my long career as a partner at several internationally prominent law firms. You will not find anyone who has done more than Jim to instill in his company's services a constant spirit and consistent practice of conscientious and compassionate excellence.

That rigorous standard applies throughout every aspect of Jim's company. All who provide service are guided by their conscience and readily undertake responsibility for doing what's right rather than what is simply expedient or merely adequate. Jennie and I were constantly impressed by this high degree of professionalism. Because Dad needed skilled nursing as well as general care, there were always two staff members staying with him, at least one of whom was a well-credentialed nurse. The shifts were staggered to enhance overlapping knowledge and awareness of his condition, thus providing better continuity of care. On several occasions over the years, a staff member's arrival at shift change was understandably delayed by weather or unforeseen developments. Despite promises from Jennie or I to remain at the house to assist the remaining nurse if needed, the caregiver scheduled to depart always courteously declined to even consider leaving until the replacement staff member arrived.

The degree of caring provided by Jim's company is wonderful. Jim and Judy each frequently stopped by to chat with Dad. Because of their work ethic, they always worked on holidays to endeavor to allow staff members some time off with their own families. We were privileged to host Jim and Judy for various holiday meals at Dad's home, "111," a popular place for decades for family and many friends to gather. However, neither Jim nor Judy would take more than a short respite from relieving their various staff members. The caring culture meant we made many new friends as well. It was a source of great pleasure to my father and our family that some of the off-duty caregivers would come to be part of the crowd gathered for holidays, birthday celebrations, and the like. As with family members and other friends, they would also simply drop by to greet Dad or, if he was napping, to enjoy strolling in his large yard and sitting a while in the garden. During one holiday meal, my father happily pointed out that there were five different languages being spoken around our large dining table, and he declared that it was like having an international club. Soon thereafter, Jennie surprised and delighted the large group of regular visitors (including Jim, Judy, and all of Dad's caregivers, of course) by distributing nice shirts marked with each recipient's name and designating each as a member of "Club 111 International." Although more than six years have passed since Dad died, we remain in touch not only with Jim and Judy but also with some of the DuPage Brightstar Care caregivers and office staff. It's always fun to see someone post a photo on Facebook showing a Club 111 shirt being worn.

The story that Jim relates in this book is, at its heart, an elegantly simple one. A nice person named Jim, who is an enthusiastic, energetic, and entrepreneurial businessperson, encounters a need to change his career path. In considering his options, Jim takes a thoughtful look at the cultural landscape. Is there an underserved need that can be fulfilled by a business conducted in a way that will be beneficial for the customer, the employees, the ownership, and the community at large? Jim realizes that the aging problem provides an excellent opportunity for just such a business. He finds that a similarly collaborative entrepreneur has developed an excellent framework for high-quality home case services in the form of the Brightstar Care franchise system. This prospect holds attractive promise. It also requires a courageous leap of faith in the face of a high-cost risk. Jim had (and has) the faith. He takes the risk and then does what he does best. The result—a huge success. How? Well, that's best learned from Jim's book.

Shooting Star doesn't just relate the joys and heartaches of the steps on the journey that comprise the story of Brightstar Care of Central DuPage-Wheaton's early days. And of course, it was not all quite that simple. Consequently, Jim's book serves multiple important purposes. I think it ought to be required reading for MBA candidates. In an entertaining manner, it is educational and inspirational. Above all, however, it is an essential guide for a growing population encountering the need for home health care. Many of us in the so-called sandwich generation, who are still happily engaged in providing varying degrees of support in our children's lives, are blessed by the presence in our lives of one or more parents who have lived beyond their prior expectations. When care is needed, the common—and very difficult—questions are "what do I do?" and "where can I find resources?" The answers are in Jim's book, gathered together and well organized in a way that is effectively unprecedented and entirely helpful. After reading the manuscript, I was reminded of a wise expression sometimes used by Ruth Golniewisz, a dear friend's mother. In the face of a complicated situation leaving others feeling unable or unsure about performing a necessary task, she would calmly point out, "Everything is easy once you know how. Don't expect yourself to automatically or already know how. Go find out how to do it. And maybe practice will be needed. But you can always find out how. And once you know how, everything is easy."

So, read Jim's book. You'll find what you need to know about how to best obtain and help to manage a loved one's home health care. You'll learn or be reminded of a few other important things as well. And I know you'll enjoy it. I sure did.

—Randy Perkins

Acknowledgments

I'd especially like to thank my wife and business partner, Judy, who joined me in starting from scratch to build something that has become truly great. None of this would have been possible without her support, medical expertise, and ability to empathize with our clients and their families. The selfless, loving standard of care she established from the beginning is simply a reflection of who and what she is.

A special callout is also necessary to the leader of our great Bright-Star Care system—Ms. Shelly Sun. She not only took a chance on Judy and me back when we all started in business together, but she lovingly, at great time expense, reviewed this book before we went to press. Her positive shadow on our business cannot be overstated.

Also, to our field and office employees, whose hard work and dedication set the mark for excellence in caregiving. Our community is benefited by their efforts.

About the Author

Jim Flickinger grew up in a small northwest Ohio farming community and attended Bowling Green State University, where he majored in food science and minored in business. After earning his bachelor of science, he completed three years of postgraduate studies at Wheaton College in Wheaton, Illinois, and at Trinity Evangelical Divinity School at Trinity International University in Deerfield, Illinois.

But his true calling was sales. After starting as a paperboy at age twelve, he came into his forte at Testing Service Corporation in Carol Stream, Illinois, where he worked his way up from a field technician to director of sales and marketing, board member, and minority owner.

Along the way, Jim indulged in his political interests, serving for more than a decade as a Milton Township (DuPage County) trustee and working on campaigns for the Forest Preserve District Board of Commissioners, the DuPage County Board chairman, the school board, US reps Randy Hultgren and Peter Roskam, and presidential candidates.

In 2008, he and his wife, Judy, established JDF Services Inc., d.b.a. BrightStar Care of Central DuPage–Wheaton. Together, they built it into a multimillion-dollar enterprise that is helping to improve the overall health of people in their service area.

Jim and Judy have been married since 1990 and have a daughter,

Aimee, who is a nurse like her mother. Aimee is married and lives in Jacksonville, Florida, with her husband, Jonathan, and twin daughters.

Jim's hobbies include cooking, gardening, home decorating, reading—especially business and self-improvement books—music, and fast cars.

Introduction

There are three touchstones to my success: my relationship with God, my marriage, and the day I started using a Franklin Planner. Back in 1977, when I got serious about my relationship with God, it changed the course and eventual outcomes of my life.

In my youth, I was irresponsible, had bad habits and friends, and was adrift. I was a mediocre student. Teachers always told my parents that I had a lot more potential than my performance and grades indicated. Truth be told, I felt unchallenged and unmotivated.

Once I established a prayerful relationship with God, I developed a strong interest in personal, intellectual, and spiritual growth that put me on a positive trajectory, leading to personal success in life. But it was my marriage to Judy and the use of that day planner that really upped my productivity and contributed to overall success.

Self-help author Napoleon Hill talks about the power of marriage enabling a couple to achieve more together than either could achieve alone, whether raising a family or building a business. When Judy and I were married on June 9, 1990, I was a field technician for Testing Service Corporation (TSC), earning about $40,000 a year. A decade later, my compensation package topped $250,000. Marriage definitely had something to do with that. The stability, support, sharing of responsibilities—you name it. There's something that went on there.

The Franklin Planner added a whole new dimension to my ability to get things done. I look through the archives now and marvel at the items I scheduled in a single day as I was preparing to plunge into my own business. I had more activities listed than there were lines in the planner. And I blasted through the stuff, sometimes thirty items a day, both personal and professional.

I always was interested in business, specifically selling, even as a little boy. As a paperboy, I always sought to be the best and frequently won trips to baseball games and other awards as a result of adding new subscribers. I also learned early on that there's a correlation between what you charge and the service people perceive they are receiving. I remember an incident that occurred while I was making my rounds collecting money from my clients. The rate was forty-two cents a week, seven cents a day. I knocked on one man's door to collect, and he said he had already paid me. He had taken forty-two pennies and thrown them over the front lawn. "That's how you delivered the paper to me last week, so that's how I am paying you!" he said. That was the first time I realized there was a correlation between service and perceived value.

We all innately perceive whether we've received value for the money we spend. For the kind of business we're in, there has to be a close correlation between perception and value for the money spent for services.

My relationship with God led me to Wheaton College in Wheaton, Illinois, a Christian liberal arts college and graduate school founded by an evangelical abolitionist about twenty-five miles west of Chicago. After I arrived in the Chicago area from the small farming community where I had grown up in northwest Ohio, I suddenly developed a host of allergies. That was in January 1982. My asthma became so severe that I had to drop my graduate work in May 1983, although by that time I had completed the coursework for a master's degree in New Testament theology. It took quite a while to get a handle on the situation. I tried again and did a year at Trinity Evangelical Divinity School in Deerfield, Illinois.

God endows each of us with special and unique talents. Some people underachieve because their talents haven't been recognized and nurtured.

Once I realized I had certain gifts and talents, I exploited and nurtured them with self-education. I never did complete grad school at Wheaton, although I had enough credits for two master's degrees. Instead, I embarked on a lifetime postgraduate reading program, averaging a book a week, with my primary interests in business and personal success and improvement. I also enjoy history, theology, philosophy, biographies, economics, and business—anything but fiction.

At Wheaton, I also learned critical thinking largely because of Dr. Arthur Rupprecht, my ancient-Greek professor. His thinking—both in the classroom and on a personal level—was so in-depth that it forced me to work harder just to try keep up with him. He was (and still is) sharp witted and cynical and brought those things out in me. We spent untold hours together engaging in his favorite hobby—fishing on Lake Michigan—and his smarts helped us catch a lot of fish in those days.

But perhaps the biggest impact his family had on me was introducing me to Judy, who had been a loving nurse for their first grandchild. We married in 1990 after dating for a year.

At the time, as I mentioned, I was a field technician for the wonderful engineering firm TSC, and I stayed with the company for twenty-four and a half years. I had become the company's director of business development by the time I left in 2009 to open BrightStar Care of Central DuPage–Wheaton.

Much of my business-management philosophy is based largely

on what I learned at TSC during nearly a quarter century with the company:

- Your profession or career should be an honorable pursuit.
- Perform your job with honesty, and strive for excellence.
- A business should have a certain family feel.
- Treat customers, employees, and vendors as you wish to be treated.
- Buy local, hire local, and contribute to local charitable causes.
- Share the fruits of success through salaries, 401(k) plans, performance bonuses, and ownership opportunities.
- There's value in longevity. Unlike corporate America, which hires people young, uses them up, and spits them out, value long-term employees for their breadth of knowledge, understanding, and dedication.
- Laissez-faire management gives your employees the ability to problem-solve on their own and become do-it-yourselfers. There simply aren't enough resources in a small business to overmanage staff.
- Owner pay need not be excessive.
- Develop a multiservice business that doesn't depend on a single revenue stream.

I left TSC because of the Great Recession, which had a profoundly negative effect on the company. TSC went from eight offices to four, and when I was told the other salesperson in our two-person department would be laid off, I decided to let him stay and instead strike out on my own.

As we looked for the right business to get into, Judy and I decided we wanted to start some type of service business that directly helped people in their homes, and going into home health care seemed the logical choice. We looked at three models—developing our own company from scratch, going with an Accessible Home Health franchise, or signing for a franchise with BrightStar Care. We chose the one that met our criteria for providing the type of honorable pursuit we could embrace. That was BrightStar Care.

The BrightStar Care service model is based on five core values:
- Being open and positive
- Serving with passion
- Always doing the right thing in an honest, ethical manner
- Doing what we say we will do
- Always striving for improvement

Our core values are what make us and our employees successful and enable our clients to thrive.

THE START OF SOMETHING BIG

We needed funding to get our BrightStar Care franchise off the ground, so I cashed in my 401(k) plan for initial working capital. That's something I never would do again, but it turned out to be money well spent.

BrightStar Franchising set us up to succeed, providing three weeks of training, encouraging us to presell the business, giving us access to various national accounts, and helping us set up a structure that has evolved into a strong organization focused on our clients' needs. There's no doubt a certain amount of luck was involved. Though the economy was in the tank, people's needs for care did not diminish, and there was a large pool of potential caregivers in the labor market.

Building JDF Services Inc., d.b.a. BrightStar Care of Central DuPage–Wheaton, was hard work, involving twelve- and sixteen-hour days—and that doesn't include the emergency calls we took after business hours. But I'd do it again in a heartbeat!

Identifying the key positions in my organization and putting the right people in those jobs has enabled me to run my business from hundreds of miles away. And giving those key people a stake in the company has allowed them to invest themselves in the operation with the hope of one day buying me out.

> If you do good, good will come back to you—sometimes in a different form and time frame.

Much of my business philosophy is rooted in Ralph Waldo Emerson's essay "Compensation," which expounds on the biblical precept of "sowing and reaping." I firmly believe in that aura: if you do good, good will come back to you—sometimes in a different form and time frame.

Napoleon Hill's views on success also have had a major impact on my thinking, especially his "mastermind" concept, which he introduced in the 1920s. The concept is based on the idea that the knowledge and effort of two or more people working in harmony toward a definite purpose creates an outcome that is greater than the individual parts. Our organization truly is more than the sum of its individual parts. For instance, one key to our success has been our relationship with Northwestern Medicine Central DuPage Hospital. It is a major source of referrals for our private-duty caregiving and nursing, as well as a key customer for our medical-staffing services.

There's no doubt that hitting breakeven in early September 2009 was a watershed moment for us. The fears of the first few months, when we were losing money, melted away, and we really got our feet under us. In those early years, our company bought out two competitors, which more than doubled our market share and augmented our staff. Setting a first-year sales record for the overall corporation was just icing on the cake.

IT'S ALL ABOUT THE PEOPLE

Before BrightStar Care, I was a sales guy, not a business manager, so I had to grow into my roles as chief financial officer and chief executive officer. As the company grew, our executive committee members also had to grow into their roles, and I have tried to lead them by example.

I always try to treat people as I want to be treated. I also believe in the power of a positive outlook to reach personal goals and look at failure as a chance to learn and improve.

As a leader, I try to inspire our employees to grow with their positions. Personal growth is important to our field staff, which is why we provide them with a plethora of continuing education units to make sure they learn new skills and brush up those skills they already have. We also encourage our caregivers to go back to school and become certified nursing assistants or track to become nurses.

Our home care service has the goal of reducing physical difficulties for our clients, keeping them safe in their homes as long as possible. Sometimes care involves nothing more than wellness checks and a few moments of companionship. Other times it involves live-in care that requires much more than just training since they are with the clients twenty-four hours a day.

At the other end of the spectrum is skilled nursing care, twenty-four hours a day for some, especially at the end of life.

Providing home care is a worthy endeavor. As a client once told me, "We will all need twenty-four-hour care at some point." Our caregivers are dedicated individuals, both those with medical licensing and those who provide companion services. Once our clients contract with us, they can be assured we will be there when they need us—both our individual clients and the institutions we staff.

The other end of our business is facilities staffing. In an assisted living facility or hospital, the nurse taking care of you or your loved one is not necessarily an employee of the facility. In our service area, that certified nursing assistant, registered nurse, or licensed practical nurse might be one of ours—and that person is no less invested in the care being provided than the facility's full-time employees.

Whatever the service, it's all about people—our staff and our clients. Our recruiting efforts are robust, but I worry about the shortage of available caregivers. One advantage the recession presented was that it was easy to hire people because so many people were out of work at that time. With the economy strengthening, the job market has tightened, helping to create a caregiver shortage, a situation that is only going to get worse as the baby boomer population continues to age. But we strive to find caregivers who are in the health care business because they want to make a positive difference in people's lives. We're constantly posting jobs on recruiting sites and continuously hiring. We carefully match clients' needs to employees' skills. Such attention to detail saves people's lives.

Our company is Joint Commission accredited, meaning we meet the highest standards of care in the industry, with our eye always on patient safety. It puts us head and shoulders above competitors who do not have Joint Commission accreditation or medical licensure. And the synergy we have with Northwestern Medicine Central DuPage Hospital and other facilities means people living in our service area are healthier and experience a higher level of care as a result.

I hope this book will give you an idea of what BrightStar Care of Central DuPage–Wheaton is about and the services we can provide for you or a loved one.

CHAPTER 1

Getting Started

No one knew it at the time, but 2007 was a watershed year. It was the start of the Great Recession. After more than thirty years of steady growth, business dried up for Testing Service Corporation (TSC), where I was in charge of sales and marketing and had been an employee for twenty-four years. Before the recession hit, TSC had been a $20 million company with eight offices around the Chicagoland region. It took a while for us to realize the Great Recession was underway and its implications.

TSC had been in business for around thirty-five years before I started working there in 1984 as a field technician, and business was booming. Employees were loyal and stuck around. Some had been there for thirty or forty years by the time I left. But we had hit a wall by Thanksgiving 2007. By the middle of 2008, I realized the situation was deteriorating. There was no work. Half of the offices were closed. Nothing was coming in. And I realized I probably would not end my career the way I had planned.

When it was suggested the company's other salesperson would soon be laid off, a light bulb went off in my head. What if I laid off myself instead of him? I had the higher salary, so it would be more beneficial for the firm.

Judy and I started batting around ideas. We had always thought about moving to Hilton Head, South Carolina, probably because we had vacationed there for many years. We had also thought about starting a business and agreed that either servicing people or maybe their homes when they were away was a good idea. Either way, a guiding principle was to help people in some fashion. Somewhere along the way, I came up with the idea of providing some kind of care in the home and ran into BrightStar Care on an internet search. I'd heard of the company before, largely from a story I'd read in Crain's Chicago Business about the founder, Shelly Sun. I began exploring the idea of becoming a BrightStar Care franchisee, and by fall 2008 I had set up a time to meet with the company.

Ninety-nine franchise units had been bought by the time Judy and I came along. We went through the application process and were approved. We made it an even one hundred after beating out two other applicants who were also interested in our territory. Today, BrightStar Franchising has sold 335 territories nationally.

Before pursuing the BrightStar Care franchise, I researched three models: BrightStar Care, Accessible Home Health Inc., and starting our own independent agency.

What I liked about BrightStar Care was its status as a non-Medicare, private-pay home care and medical-staffing service. What makes us unique is that we supply skilled medical services in states where we can get skilled-care licenses. That puts us miles ahead of agencies that don't offer skilled nursing.

At the time, potential franchisees met with Shelly in a "Discovery Day" format at the company headquarters in Gurnee, Illinois. Judy had not planned on getting involved in the business. She just tagged along to the meeting to see "what Jim was getting himself into."

I went into the meeting with Shelly well prepared. I knew she was a University of Tennessee graduate and brought her a gift of the school's tchotchkes featuring the big orange T. They were a big hit.

More importantly, I brought a guest book Judy and I had kept at our home. When we invited people over, we would have them sign it. We had only been in the house for five years, but we had accumulated more than one thousand signatures in that time from overnight guests, engineering/business parties, political fund-raisers, and other events. We had signatures from a pair of congressmen, Randy Hultgren and Peter Roskam, who still serve in the US Congress, and the mayor of Wheaton had signed it. I think that's what put our bid over the top, showing Shelly that we had deep local roots in our community and could get things done.

Before making it official, I contacted other franchisees to get their take on the company. I came away really impressed with the quality of the people involved in BrightStar Care, both the franchisees and corporate staff we had met. In fact, I asked Shelly whether her franchisees were already good when they got involved or whether they had grown to that level with their BrightStar Care businesses. I concluded that it takes a certain level of confidence and competence to take on the BrightStar Care model. You grow and learn really fast, or you don't survive. Judy and I and our staff look back and marvel at how we've grown personally as a result of our involvement.

> BrightStar Care's high best practices and the depth of support blew the others away. It was so self-evident.

After the meeting at BrightStar Care, we headed to Florida to meet with the Accessible Home Health people. Because we had the interviews within days of each other, we were in a position to make instant comparisons. BrightStar Care's high best practices and the depth of support blew the others away. It was so self-evident. It did not take long to realize we were dealing with very bright people, both on the franchisor and franchisee side of things, and they had very sophisticated systems in place to leverage our success.

BrightStar Care did not offer us the franchise immediately, but Shelly did convince Judy that if I was awarded the franchise, she should be involved. After all, she was a nurse—albeit pediatric—and her skill set would be invaluable. Shelly told us it would be about ten days before the decision was made among the various applicants for our territory. Accessible Home Health did make us an immediate offer. We said we would consider it, then headed for Hilton Head for a two-week family vacation.

Before the first week was out, we received a call from BrightStar Care and were told we had been selected! BrightStar Franchising over-nighted the documents to us, and we executed them November 10, 2008, from Hilton Head.

I didn't terminate my position at TSC immediately. Instead, I went in and talked with my boss to work out an arrangement that enabled me to use vacation time to push my departure date to January 2009 so that I could take advantage of a stock repurchase option.

TOO NAIVE TO BE TERRIFIED

BrightStar Care provided three weeks of intensive preopening training. From the time that ended on January 22, 2009, until we officially opened our office March 9, I went into a preopening sales frenzy. I made more than five hundred contacts, literally hitting every nook and cranny of our territory, weekdays and weekends, day and night. I destroyed two pairs of dress shoes in the slush and salt that winter!

At our BrightStar Care training, Shelly had said, "You only have one chance to presell your business. Then you open your doors, and that chance is gone forever." The nice thing about the health care community is that it's deferential and an easier sales process than many business types. People are casual about walk-in sales calls and usually are not harsh if you don't know all the answers. Just like us, they are in the people-service business—specifically, caring for their clients' health.

But initially, things were very discouraging, and that was pretty humbling for a guy who had been a sales star in his previous position. I had made multimillions of dollars in sales for twenty years at TSC. Now, in my own business, I was striking out. Day after day, and after many, many sales calls, I seemingly was not able to get the phone to ring back at the office. I was quite frustrated, but we simply had to make it work. I had invested our life savings by using my 401(k) (which had been cut in half by the stock market crash) as seed capital in the business. Breakeven for our BrightStar Care franchise was about $12,000 a week, but for the first few weeks, we had no billables at all to speak of.

It wasn't that we didn't have any clients. We did have a few, which we inherited from neighboring BrightStar Care franchisees that had been servicing our open territory. Judy had a patient load of three or four by the third week. We also benefited from BrightStar Care's national accounts program, where we provide local staffing for such things as specialty infusion pharmacies and employee-assistance companies providing backup care as part of some corporate employee benefits packages: if a child gets sick, the parent can call for a caregiver so he or she doesn't miss a day of work. When we opened, we got a lot of support from two neighboring franchisees, Jim Guzdziol in the Naperville–Oak Brook area and Tom Koenig to the north. Koenig, in particular, was most helpful, lending us his accountant, Don Forlani, so that our finances were correct right from the get-go.

In July, I hired a second salesperson, family friend Leonard Sanchez, and then brought over a lady from TSC in a lateral position for office operational help. It did not take long for Sanchez to bring in our first twenty-four-hour client, and from there things really took off. We broke even at week twenty-one in business and wound up breaking BrightStar Care's first-year sales record.

Since then, we have been awarded nearly every BrightStar Care system award: we have forty-eight excellence awards, including all the big ones like system-wide Nurse of the Year, Regional Caregiver of the Year, Franchisee of the Year, and Mentor of the Year. We've also been recognized for marketing, online reputation, and clinical and operational excellence. Before the end of the first year, we had so many patients, we brought on Kelly Honn as our assistant director of nursing. She had been working for us as a field nurse at the time and took over as director of nursing when Judy officially retired in 2014.

We took on our first patient while operating out of cramped offices in a basement. I shared an office with our assistant director of nursing, JoAnn Finlon, who had helped open two other BrightStar Care offices in the area. Judy had begged her to join us. One day, I heard her half of a phone conversation and afterward asked her what was going on. "Oh, our caregiver just arrived at Ms. Helen's home, and she has fallen again. I'm going over there [she lived very nearby] to help out," she responded.

This was eye opening for me. "What kind of business did I get us involved in?" I asked myself. I had come from the engineering field. Engineers and their work are very methodical and orderly. Things ran predictably, staid, and mostly kind of boring. Now I owned a business beset by some level of chaos, or the threat of such, most all the time! That event was far from isolated. It was a difficult adjustment for me in the first couple of years. But over time I learned that by accepting and handling the chaos, we were serving our beloved patients and providing that peace of mind we promised their family members, which is why they invited us into their homes in the first place! That's the nature of health care. Just think about the number of television shows based on the drama in hospital emergency rooms. Still, I'm not blasé about it, and it is something I would warn prospective franchisees about. You just never quite fully adapt to the chaotic incomings that make up a typical day in the wonderful world of health care.

Judy panicked a little when we first started. She had been a pediatric nurse for forty years and was nervous about caring for patients at the other end of the age spectrum. However, her training transferred quite nicely to geriatric care. She has a sweet, loving nature and is roundly adored by all. Cheri McEssy, a lady who owned several other BrightStar Care franchises in the area, helped Judy get up to speed on home care nursing. She had been in charge of an entire floor at Children's Memorial Hospital and was on duty in the pediatric intensive care unit when Y2K hit. It was her job to make sure the ventilators and other equipment stayed on in case the click-over to 2000 proved disastrous. It didn't. We were lucky to have people like that help us get on our feet.

Judy never really planned to be involved in BrightStar Care. She had been working in a pediatrician's office at the time and planned to continue doing that on a part-time basis. It was Shelly Sun who slowly convinced her that she could help me. She started by asking Judy if she could give shots. When she answered yes, Sun asked Judy if she could do assessments. Yes again. The questions went on like that until Judy concluded she'd be an asset.

It's no secret that if a married couple are going to work together, they need to be involved in different and separate aspects of the business. In our case, I handled the sales and business end of things; Judy handled the care management and the clinical side of things. We complemented each other, and just about the only conflicts that arose were when I tried to get involved in something clinical or Judy would try to give me business advice. As long as we kept to our own areas of expertise, we got along famously—we really did!

> As long as we kept to our own areas of expertise, we got along famously— we really did!

We routinely worked twelve- to sixteen-hour days, seven days a week, and took no vacations for the first two and half years. It is BrightStar Care's rule that the phone be answered 24-7-365, so we took all the on-call for the business for the first three years or so.

Would I do it all again? You bet I would, in a heartbeat. Bright-

Star Care's systems and support are so deep and substantial, and the training is so comprehensive; there's no comparison among competitors. Our family, employees, and client families that we have touched are so much better off because we applied this BrightStar Care system in our local marketplace.

HOW BRIGHTSTAR CARE SET US UP FOR SUCCESS

BrightStar Care's support included providing us with ten large operations manuals, covering everything from leasing office space to accounting to scheduling—there's an entire tome on sales and marketing. BrightStar Care's help also included business insurance. That's huge in this business. We franchisees receive premium pricing from our vendors because BrightStar Care is buying quantity in massive groups. BrightStar Care also provides payroll services through Automatic Data Processing Inc., for a fraction of the price small businesses generally pay.

BrightStar Care's proprietary computer software program provides everything we need to operate our business, including all the human resources materials we need for such things as applicant processing and hiring, as well as credentialing and maintenance of credentials. When you have three hundred employees, that's a massive headache out of the way.

Regional field representatives also provide support. BrightStar Care really invests heavily in franchisees up front so it can reap the royalties later as the business becomes successful.

It's like Ralph Waldo Emerson's essay "Compensation": "The absolute balance of Give and Take, the doctrine that everything has its price, --and if that price is paid, not that thing but something else is obtained, and that it is impossible to get anything without its price."[1]

The essay itself expands on the biblical principle of the law of reaping and sowing: you get from life what you've given, both the positive and negative. You cannot be successful if you haven't paid the proper price. I look at the positive side of the equation. We do things others would never do so that we attain the things others never will have. I pay my bills on time—sometimes ahead of time—hoping my clients will do likewise. Cheap materials yield cheap products, so we err on the side of quality, treating our employees as we would like to be treated.

BrightStar Care has annual conferences: one for office staff and the other for owners. These are three- to four-day affairs where we are updated on system matters and share best practices. We also have regional franchisee summits where we share concerns and practices with one another. And then there's the Chicagoland co-op just for those of us in the Chicagoland area.

The care BrightStar Care of Central DuPage–Wheaton provides clients runs the gamut from companion or simple home care services all the way up to personal care provided by a certified nursing assistant and skilled home nursing care provided by a licensed practical nurse or a registered nurse. Also, we got into medical-staffing services very early on.

Customer and employee satisfaction surveys also are a big part of our operation. An outside agency, Home Care Pulse, conducts them monthly, querying 10 percent of our patients and our field staff. In fact, we've had complaints that we survey too much! We received their Employer and Provider of Choice awards for 2018.

---

1   Ralph Waldo Emerson, "Compensation," *American Transcendentalism Web*, accessed April 4, 2019, https://archive.vcu.edu/english/engweb/transcendentalism/authors/emerson/essays/compensation.html.

CHAPTER 2

Getting to the Top

The idea of starting a new business during a major recession might seem crazy, but really, we didn't have a choice. Besides, it was some time before we realized exactly how bad the economic downturn was to become. Maybe in this instance ignorance was bliss!

TSC was hit really hard. The company had three revenue streams, and the two of them that were heavily dependent on new project development in the private sector were suffering. The preconstruction services / preliminary soils investigation and environmental site assessments virtually dried up by the end of 2007. The construction-materials testing and engineering continued through 2008 because of projects that had started construction or were funded and needed to be completed. But once they were done, that work dried up as well. Work in the public sector continued somewhat through the recession. In fact, that was about the only work that was left. By the time I left, the company had shrunk to about half its former size. That was about eighteen months into the recession.

As I began researching the business possibilities out there, it seemed to me that health care showed the most promise for establishing a stable operation that would meet our criteria for helping others and doing something honorable. I went back and reread the article on BrightStar Care that I had seen in Crain's Chicago Business.

Judy and I liked the idea of serving people in their homes. We could feel good at the end of the day helping people.

We really didn't pay much attention to the recession as we went about building the business, but we did sense its impact as we entered people's homes. We would get calls, usually from the patient's family, and were often surprised by the depth of the loved one's care needs. Once we went out to do the assessments and provided cost estimates, many times the families would say they could not afford us. We were—and still are—strictly private pay. That means no help from Medicare or gap coverage to help defray the costs. It was heartbreaking. Just because the families couldn't afford our services, their need did not go away. Many of these people needed help with such basic things as getting out of bed in the morning, personal grooming, and care. We didn't even know where we could refer people that we could not help.

> Just because the families couldn't afford our services, their need did not go away.

With Medicare coverage getting tighter and tighter, less and less is going to be covered. Presently, it does not cover custodial care, which is the term used to describe our services. Such incidents convinced Judy and me that we needed to buy long-term-care (LTC) insurance policies. Right now, that is the only insurance that completely covers basic personal-care and activities-of-daily-living needs. It probably is too late for our parents' generation, but we have urged any other baby boomers to do the same thing—even though only one in twenty people who are covered with LTC insurance will ever use it. But that one who qualifies for LTC benefits will really need it.

PRESELLING THE BUSINESS

You have only one chance to presell your business. Then
you open up, and that chance is gone forever!

—Shelly Sun, BrightStar Care CEO

Previous to BrightStar Care, my sales experience was business to business. Selling health care was going to be really different.

When you're selling to businesses, as I did in the engineering world, there's a structure. Meetings are scheduled so you can get to the decision maker straight out of the box.

Selling health care services was the opposite: cold-calling door-to-door.

The guidance I got from Shelly Sun at our preopening training was that the industry was more relaxed since, by definition, it was centered around helping the patient. Walk-ins were acceptable and informal. Maybe you'd get to meet with someone; maybe not. It was easy entry, but it lacked depth. They'd be friendly and meet, but no sale would result.

When you're preselling in this industry, potential clients cut you slack. They realized I was still learning the business. I made five hundred of those sales calls before we opened—without any immediate results.

But I like people and like talking. Selling is in my blood. I was selling goods and services that were needed, honorable, and truthfully represented. That made all that work pleasurable and worthwhile, even though it meant slogging through the slush before winter gave way to spring and we officially opened our doors.

What was tough in the beginning was that we were totally unknown in our locale and had to build our brand recognition from the ground up. It helped that there were other BrightStar Care franchises in the Chicago area, so the BrightStar Care name wasn't completely unknown, but it was not a household name in those early days.

The advice given by marketing guru Dan Kennedy proved quite helpful in those early days. One of Kennedy's principles is that, no matter what the national model is, brand recognition and reputation are built at the local level. Having marketing and a full-time salesperson are key.

> If you can't be proud of what you're selling, you shouldn't be selling it. Go find something honorable to promote.

I kept my eye on the fact that we would be assisting people. We would be providing people with basic needs for daily living and in some cases keeping them alive. We would also be helping businesses by providing them with staffing. It was something someone with the most sensitive conscience could be proud to do. If you can't be proud of what you're selling, you shouldn't be selling it. Go find something honorable to promote.

Over time, I began to realize that my shotgun approach to sales was pretty ineffective and not the best use of my time. That was a little painful for someone who subscribes to Kennedy's time-management principle: "Time Truth #1—if you don't know what your time is worth, you can't expect the world to know it either."[2] In other words, if you have lack of respect for your time, the world will oblige by wasting even more of it. In those early days, we simply did not have

---

2   Dan Kennedy, *No B.S. Time Management for Entrepreneurs: The Ultimate No Holds Barred Kick Butt Take No Prisoners Guide to Time Productivity and Sanity* (Irvine, CA: Entrepreneur Press, 2017).

the luxury of wasted time and efforts. Our survival depended on being more efficient with our time, so I refined my sales approach until it was much more targeted.

It also helped that we began to build a reputation from servicing the patients whom neighboring BrightStar Care franchisees and national accounts referred to us, and that's when the office phones started ringing.

IT'S A REFERRAL BUSINESS

I never planned to get involved in a business that required a double sale, but that's exactly what this business entails. First, we have to convince our health care referral partners that we are the best home care option in our marketplace; then, if we do that, the referral partner refers us to a family, and we have to convince the family also, as the end user.

Our business really is conducted through referrals, whether from the hospital and other health care providers or from satisfied clients or their families. It's a two-tiered sale.

Word-of-mouth referrals are probably the most effective means of marketing. When we started, since we were unknown, there was no word-of-mouth activity for us. Fortunately, after we had successfully provided care for a number of patients, word of mouth took over, and we weren't so dependent on marketing and sales. About a third of our new business comes from word of mouth.

That's how this business is sold—or not. And I'm not just talking about individual cases here. Word-of-mouth patients can come through our major referral sources as well.

HOME CARE SERVICES

One of the keys to our success was our relationship with Central DuPage Hospital. The hospital had a large presence in the homes in our territory through its home health agency. Home health is typically an in-home medical service that is covered by Medicare. It usually involves skilled nursing care or other therapy for specific illnesses, injuries, or posthospital discharge. We are not a home health agency, per se, but we are licensed and competent to provide skilled nursing services, which are similar in nature to home health but are privately paid rather than Medicare.

Central DuPage Hospital provided home health services through its CNS Home Health & Hospice organization (now Northwestern Medicine Home Health & Hospice). The organization, founded in 1955, defined home health care and hospice services in our region. It was typically staffed by nurses who lived nearby their patients in our community. It also had a large, adjunct, private-duty operation called Caring Choices.

When making my early sales rounds, I had lunch one day with the DuPage County treasurer, Gwen Henry, who is a business-minded friend and wanted to encourage us starting out in business. She had been on the hospital board and just blurted out, "Jim, what are you going to do about CNS?" I knew what she was asking about. Our business was a miniscule upstart and CNS/Caring Choices and the hospital had been steadfastly caring for the needs of our area long before we came along. I did not have an answer. I told her, "Gwen, I don't know what we will do about CNS, but I will have to figure it out." There were really only one of two ways it could go: CNS could stymie our growth, or, better yet, we could develop a working relationship with them, if possible. I had tried to make some calls to

CNS, but they wouldn't let me in the door. I was at a loss to develop an approach.

The light bulb came on during a second sales call to one of our competitors, Comfort Keepers in Addison, Illinois. The receptionist, who had recognized me from the initial sales call, was in the parking lot taking a smoke break, and we started talking it up. She noted that we could provide medical services, something Comfort Keepers was unable to do. When CNS had more incoming new patients than it could handle, it made calls to other companies to help with its overflow. Comfort Keepers wasn't equipped to take the cases that required medical personnel, but we were, and that gave me an idea for a starting point with CNS.

A short time later, I attended a function where Sue Levitt, the executive director of CNS, was making a presentation to a group of seniors. She and I got to talking after the event, and when I told her what we were doing, she responded that we'd have to get together. That's all I needed to hear.

Shortly after that, Judy and I met with Levitt in her office. I got the feeling during that meeting that Sue innately sensed that Judy and I were "the real deal" and she was willing to take a chance on us. She invited Caring Choices director Nancy Houser into the meeting. At the time, Houser was looking to expand Caring Choices but was at the point where she couldn't take any more cases because of staffing limitations. We worked out a deal where we could help staff her overflow operations. Caring Choices even provided our people with their top-notch training. It was a win-win: she could put the revenue on her books, and we grew our client base—albeit short-term cases because many of the patients had been discharged home to hospice. Some patients, though, required months of care—and BrightStar Care supplied it whenever we were asked.

We ran our service model operations 24-7, which meant we answered the phones twenty-four hours a day, seven days a week. So we were particularly helpful to Caring Choices after hours and on weekends, and the arrangement was really a great benefit to our mutual patients. They were receiving the best quality care from hospital to home. If a patient could pay for it, that patient was getting the best-of-the-best service.

Again, I want to stress, we did not (and still do not) provide home health or hospice services, which are covered by Medicare. When we would receive an inquiry for such services, we would refer the caller to CNS, and that is still our policy. We did not want to horn in on their business or duplicate what they were already doing quite effectively—especially given the level at which they provide such services.

Eventually management at CNS changed. The agency decided to redouble its emphasis on its core competencies of home health and hospice services. As a result, it dropped the private-duty business, Caring Choices. The operation then transferred all its patients who were willing to do so to our care. That's when our BrightStar Care business had a more direct connection to the hospital and better served its discharged patients.

In 2012, CNS decided to start providing continuous nursing care for its hospice patients. This is a Medicare-paid service for those patients who are deemed as needing full-time nursing care at end of life. CNS decided to add that to its list of services but contracted with us to provide the nurses to staff it. This also benefited our BrightStar Care neighboring franchisees, who staffed continuous-care patients for CNS in the surrounding areas.

One Easter weekend, we had three continuous-care cases going, and a fourth was called in. We had to refer that last case out to one of our BrightStar Care neighbors since we had reached our max.

To forge such a good working relationship with an organization of the professional depth as CNS so early in our business life was an incredible opportunity. The kindness and professional courtesy they showed to us during that time of vulnerability for us must have been providential. Who knows where we would have gone without that key relationship? In those early days, at times it represented up to half of our business volume. In addition, we grew in leaps and bounds by being associated with the high practices of this experienced local health care provider. We looked in awe at their professionalism in the homes and took it all in. To this day, we still enjoy a great relationship with CNS.

> When it comes to private-duty services, you simply cannot miss a shift.

At any time, we can be taking care of twenty-five to fifty patients referred to us from the hospital or home health agency. This represents a large chunk of the 180 or so active clients on our books, so nurturing and maintaining a great relationship with our local hospital and home health agency is extremely important, especially to the mutual clients that we serve in our community.

In addition to CNS, in the early days, we got the bulk of our referrals for new patients from Windsor Park Manor, a continuing care retirement community in Carol Stream, Illinois, and from Marianjoy Rehabilitation Hospital and Clinics.

When it comes to private-duty services, you simply cannot miss a shift. If you do, you're putting the patient at risk. When a new client comes in, our nurse-management staff has to put together a care plan, assessing the services needed and matching those to our caregivers. Then the caregivers have to be scheduled to provide those services in the most effective manner possible. Showing up for the shift, understanding and following the care plan, and communication between shifts are essential for the client's well-being.

From the very start, we marketed both private-duty services in the home and medical-staffing services for facilities. But initially our business was almost exclusively in the home with private-duty clients. I continue to encourage all BrightStar Care franchisees to get involved in staffing services due to the diversity and breadth it brings to the business, but the volume of work that comes from staffing can be unpredictable and sometimes choppy. Institutions tend to call us when they perceive they will be short staffed and then understandably cancel shifts because their own people have opted to fill the work.

Our medical-staffing clients are mostly skilled nursing facilities. We have a very effective recruiting regime and are basically a medical-staffing placement agency. We tend to function as their overflow provider in most instances. The difference between us and other competing staffing service companies is that just like with our private-duty clients, we try to fill every shift and provide premium service as well. Financially, it makes more sense for these facilities and even hospitals to fill a large portion of their staffing needs with their own personnel and then contract out for the rest. That way they're not overstaffed during lulls.

Our private-duty / staffing mix is about 65 percent / 35 percent right now. It's been as high as 50/50. In addition, we're currently providing staffing to virtually every school district, private school, and skilled nursing facility in our area. With the schools, we are providing specialized one-on-one nursing for their medically special-needs students.

SCARY TIMES

The first few months in this business were frightening. We were losing money week by week and were nowhere near the $12,000 a week in billings we needed to get to breakeven. Judy and I weren't taking salaries, and we were more than a little concerned we might not make it.

Then one day we got a knock on the door from the financial planner who had an office upstairs in our building. He said he needed help for his parents, mainly his father. It was humbling to see people we knew on a personal level trusting us enough to place the care of their loved ones into our hands. It still remains such an honor yet a very sobering responsibility. There simply is no place for failure in this trust model.

Our fifth patient was our first live-in case. The woman was ninety-six years old at the time and still driving! But time catches up with us all. They made her take the driver's license test every year at that age, and when she turned ninety-eight, she failed it. To add insult to injury, when she went outside after failing her test, she found that a sixteen-year-old who had just gotten his license had hit her car. She lamented to me that "2011 had not been a good year" because (1) her dishwasher died and had to be replaced, (2) she lost her driver's license, and (3) that year, her family made her take a live-in caregiver seven days a week. We had been there weekdays, and she had been able to be on her own for the weekends up to that point. Fortunately for her, 2012 and 2013 were better years since we were privileged to join the family in celebrating her one hundredth birthday in a gala event in mid-2013.

Another early patient was a retired business owner in Lombard. We had cared for his wife after she was hospitalized and then was released back home to hospice care. By the time he called me, he was in a wheelchair, and his cancer had come back with a vengeance. Though Judy and the other nurses handled his wife's care, this time he wanted to talk to me. It was two crusty businessmen talking straight. Even though he was wheelchair bound, we went outside to a huge storage building behind the house, where he showed me his antique-truck collection. It was amazing. One was an old steel tanker delivery truck with wooden side racks. He had pictures made up of that jewel and gave me one. I kept it under the glass on my desk for many years after that.

We were hovering at $10,000 a week by the first week in July, four months after opening our doors. We had twenty active clients, largely inherited from neighboring BrightStar Care franchisees and from BrightStar Care's national accounts program, when we got our first twenty-four-hour patient. That means full-time bedside care for two twelve-hour shifts each day, seven days a week. Over the course of a 168-hour week, that involves up to six or seven people to provide service in order to mitigate overtime. True twenty-four-hour care differs from live-in care. Live-in service means someone is on the premises twenty-four hours a day, but the caregivers have time to sleep and personal time off as well.

That first twenty-four-hour patient was also our initial exposure to amyotrophic lateral sclerosis (ALS), commonly called Lou Gehrig's disease, which is a neurodegenerative disease that affects nerve cells in the brain and spinal cord and leads to muscle weakness and paralysis.[3] The patient remains mentally acute as the body slowly expires. This patient was in a wheelchair and practically incapacitated. His wife was devastated. At one point, he demanded a meeting to give his input about our services. He was put off by the number of people involved who were showing up at his home. He realized he was our biggest client, and, in a meeting with Judy and me, he demanded our best. I said, "OK." We were with that dear family until the end.

From there, we never looked back. By October 1, we were at $20,000 a week and then doubled the billing again by October 10. At that point, we had started to do some medical staffing as well.

IT'S MORE THAN JUST SELLING

The road to success encompasses more than just selling. You should not just constantly ask from the community without giving back. We look at the needs of our clients—both individuals and institutional operations—and try to do just that, first through our care but also through targeted opportunities to financially give back.

By mid-2009, I realized CNS had a large hospice volunteer organization. In several situations, we were working side by side with its volunteers in the home. As such, we became aware that this organization had needs that we were perfectly suited to meet. Though we were not yet at breakeven, our business wrote a $1,000 check specifically to

---

3   "Symptoms and Diagnosis," ALS Association, accessed July 10, 2019, http://www.
      alsa.org/about-als/symptoms.html.

meet needs the volunteer organization would experience in the homes of its hospice patients. We did the same thing very early at Marianjoy. At times, our charitable donations represented more than 10 percent of our profits—sort of on the tithing principle. The donation amounts in those early days were so large they were too much for our accountant to deduct on our income taxes. In the last several years, as the business has grown, the total giving has incrementally increased, and the practice of giving back to our community is an embedded part of our culture.

2

CHAPTER 3

Growing the Business

Not much else matters when you're starting a business until you get to breakeven, and we managed that in early July 2009. Things really were falling into place, and people were taking notice. There are two ways to grow your client base and increase market share: emphasize continued sales growth or buy a competitor. We did both.

In mid-August, a few weeks after hitting that breakeven milestone, I got a call from a competitor, Nat Truitt, who was running an independent caregiving service in the area, Always There Resources.

It was his second venture into caregiving. He had been associated with another franchisor and didn't like the way it was run, so he had sold out, agreeing to a five-year noncompete clause. He had dabbled in a few other businesses, but when the noncompete ran out, he decided to get back into caregiving.

Then we showed up. He was concerned because he saw home care services shifting to a higher degree of medical acuity, and since we were licensed to provide skilled medical services in the home, it could present a business model problem for him.

We had originally met at an Association of Senior Service Providers of DuPage County function. I already knew of him since he had been in business locally for several years prior to our meeting. After that, I paid calls to his office, so we were already on friendly terms when he called me up one day with an invitation to have lunch. He broached the subject of our BrightStar Care business buying him out. "We're nonmedical," he said, "and you've got medical licensure. We don't want to get it, and over time, that's going to make a big difference." Truth to tell, despite our medical licensure and competencies, his business didn't look all that different from ours. We both had about the same number of clients, field employees, pricing, case management, and similar care models. I told him I was interested.

He was operating in Glen Ellyn, Illinois, an area where we had had a hard time making inroads, largely because of his presence. At the time, we were billing about $15,000 to $16,000 a week compared to his $20,000 or so. After that initial conversation, I took a week for due diligence. I learned he ran a high-quality operation and had a healthy mix of live-in and regular home care cases—thirty-five or thirty-six in all—and forty-five employees. It was kind of miraculous what a good fit it was, and I was ready to buy.

We started talking price and came up with a number. In early September, however, he started wavering, saying he wasn't sure he really wanted to sell his "baby." He had lovingly built that business quite well, as an independent operator, I might add. Then there were a couple of weeks where sales were on-again, off-again. Then, he reached out and told me that he just could not do it.

At that point, we scheduled another lunch, and I did not disguise my feelings about the road we had traveled to get to a point of "no deal." I told him he shouldn't engage in these kinds of discussions if he wasn't serious. I told him I was still willing to pay him good money, but I didn't appreciate having my time wasted. At that point, however, it was pretty obvious we could build the business by the regular means of providing great service and superb marketing and sales. I told him I'd be successful with or without him.

And that was it for several weeks.

Then on a Monday, September 28, 2009, I got an email from him. The subject line read: "Are you feeling spontaneous?" He wanted to set up another lunch, and he was ready to sell. What had happened in the intervening weeks was that he had seen his billings go down by about 20 percent. We had flipped positions: he was billing about $15,000 to $18,000 a week, and we were at $20,000 or $22,000 and continuing a strong growth track.

Shortly thereafter, we signed a purchase agreement, and on October 2, we signed the final documents. Our BrightStar Care business assumed his patients and employees officially on October 5. He was paid twenty times his weekly billings ($17,100, based on a two-week average when we took over), with him financing a good portion of the purchase price for 0 percent for three years. About halfway through the financing, he asked for the balance to be paid in full because he wanted the money to invest in another venture. We were in a position to do that, so I said sure—for a price. He wasn't too happy about having to discount the balance to get his money.

Always There came with two care managers in addition to the field personnel and clients. Virtually all of its clients came over to us, including one who was outside our franchise territory in Downers Grove. When you're part of a franchise organization, you can't infringe on the territory of a fellow franchisee. So I went to the neighboring franchisee and explained the situation. Luckily for us, she said we could keep the client and provide service in her business area. Nine years later, we are still providing service to that extraordinarily lengthy live-in client. We also still employ several of the employees that transferred over to us in 2009.

To recap, at week thirty after our opening, we absorbed a business that was roughly our size, which effectively doubled our size instantly, including clients, field employees, and patient-management staff. When we started our agency, we were BrightStar Care franchise number one hundred, meaning ninety-nine other territories had been sold prior to ours. Understandably, since we had just started, we were right at the bottom, or number one hundred in our sales level. Because of the Always There acquisition, by the middle of October 2009, week thirty-two in business, we were billing at number two in the system. That did get some attention within the BrightStar Care system.

In addition to running Always There Resources, Truitt had a medical-alarm business, which we purchased separately for $75,000 about five or six months later. It was a pretty neat little system that, at one point, had 170 clients. The system includes a speaker and a microphone, and with the press of a button, the client is connected to a responder who asks, "Hi, Mrs. So-and-So. Are you OK?" Though the bulk of the calls aren't life-threatening emergencies, we've received letters from clients' families saying their mothers are alive because of that button. It can really be a lifesaver.

We had one client who fell facedown in his yard and couldn't get back up the front steps. It was raining, and the poor guy was just lying there. Even though the system wasn't designed to work outside the home, he was wearing his medical-alarm button, and he pressed it. He told me, "When I heard those sirens, I knew who they were coming for!" Another time, I was driving around, and I spotted one of our clients in his garage with his brother. I stopped to pay a friendly visit. As we were shooting the breeze, I noticed he didn't have his button on. I outed him for that and told his brother to make sure he wears it. In an emergency, it won't help if you are not wearing the button, I told him.

We had one patient who had previously fallen down the stairs to the basement, and the family had been concerned for some time that it might happen again. We hooked up the alarm so that it would go off whenever the basement door was opened. There was never another basement-stairway incident for him.

With the expansion of cellular service, however, the original medical-alarm system, which connects to a landline, is now somewhat obsolete. Also, the button doesn't work if the patient is out of range of the receiver. It's better to teach a senior how to use a cell phone these days.

The alarm worked well for families that could not afford the amount of care the patient actually needed. The service can help bridge the gap, especially at night when a patient has to get up to go to the bathroom and may fall in the dark. It can make a difference in whether the patient can stay in his or her home. We had a family in Glen Ellyn who had a caregiver come in for a few hours a day, but all too often, our caregiver would arrive to find the patient on the floor, unable to get up. The woman needed a lot more help than she was getting.

There are situations where a medical alarm can really be lifesaving. It was wonderful technology for its time, and we still have a handful of clients with the service. But we rarely sign up anyone new and don't push it because of the other technologies that are available. As I write this, we only bill $120 a quarter for the service, less than $500 a year. Overall, it's a very small part of our business, less than $100 a week at a time when our total weekly billings were about $135,000 per week.

Integrating Always There Resources with our operation was simple since the businesses were so similar and they were well run. The one thing BrightStar Care did differently was to constantly survey patients and employees to gauge how they felt about the service. Through those surveys, we found that patients were happy with the transition to

BrightStar Care, especially since we left rates as they were. Over time, our prices have gone up to keep up with raising wages.

Later in our business life, April 2012, we bought a second local home care operation—Symmetry Home Care. I knew the owner from my time at TSC. She had been in sales for Lakewood Homes, a large local residential developer. But when the downturn hit in 2008, she was without a job, so she started Symmetry. The company did pretty well, but it wasn't as well run as Always There Resources or our BrightStar Care business, and her caregivers weren't as loyal. As a result, we paid less on a per-sales-volume basis for her agency.

When we initially discussed the purchase of her business, she was billing about $25,000 a week. By the time we reached an agreement, her billings had dwindled, in part because some of her clients and caregivers had made private arrangements with one another. We finally agreed that the purchase price would be a multiple of twenty times their final weekly sales amount ($10,000), totaling $200,000. I asked her for the same favorable terms I had gotten from Truitt. She agreed. A short time later, I heard she was starting another business and offered to give her the balance for a discounted price. Her accountant OK'd it, and I wrote her a check.

HOW WE FIT INTO THE BRIGHTSTAR CARE MODEL

Currently, there are 335 territories and 186 BrightStar Care owners. Many locations are run by franchisees that run multiple locations, and the franchisor has always maintained at least one company-owned location.

The very first BrightStar Care was founded and operated by Shelly Sun and her salesman husband, J. D. Sun. They had conceived the premium home care idea when trying to find care for his grandmother in Florida. They wanted the best for her but found the services they looked at to be wanting—hence the idea of a premium home care service model, BrightStar Care, was born. Their first area of operations was Lake County (Gurnee), Illinois.

J. D. Sun is a consummate sales guy and set a first-year sales mark of $1,093,591. That amount of business in an initial year is remarkable considering, unlike the rest of us franchisees, they did not have a business model to follow to support that level of sales. All the activities that go with servicing that amount of business were developed back at the office primarily by Shelly Sun. In addition, they needed to get it right if they were going to have a duplicable, scalable model that subsequent franchisees like ours could follow. It was clearly a remarkable first-year feat on their part. After putting the Gurnee office on the map, Shelly proceeded to assemble teams and open two more Chicagoland BrightStar Care offices—one in Chicago and the other in McHenry County.

That first-year sales record held up at $1,093,591 until we came along. By the time our first year ended, we had record sales of $1,115,391, beating the old record by $21,800. That represented about two-thirds of a week's sales. Here's a little secret about that first-year—we had fifty-three billing periods instead of the usual fifty-two. That little quirk in the calendar comes around every eight-and-a-half years and it hit just right for our first year. We needed that extra week or we would not have taken the number-one spot! And, unlike the original founders, we had the advantage

> By the time our first year ended, we had record sales of $1,115,391, beating the old record by $21,800.

of their system guiding us and a field director who proved a very good coach. He was our biggest cheerleader. We also got great support from then–BrightStar Care president Chuck Bailey. In a previous business life, Chuck had been involved in a lot of mergers and acquisitions. He generously gave his considerable advice during the Always There purchase. Based on his help, I went forward with that deal.

When we hit our one-year record, our field director suggested a party. The Suns, along with most of the senior management team of the franchisor, met us at Gibsons Bar & Steakhouse in Rosemont for a night of sales celebration. As the story goes, our field director really wanted to crown Judy and me as royalty with silver crowns for the event. After he flew into Chicago, he looked high and low for some sort of crowns befitting a queen and king, but to no avail. He ended up at a local Burger King, snagged a couple of cardboard crowns and wrapped them in tin foil so he could crown us at the dinner table! He even brought a cake with an inscription in frosting. It was a nice evening.

We were in such a good spot, I was sure 2010 was going to be even more spectacular. And it was. Our second year was on steroids. We had ended our first year billing $40,000 to $42,000 a week. One week in January, we hit $55,107, so there was an "aura" that the whole year would be great.

It took some effort to absorb the volume on a service basis, but we didn't sit back on our laurels and decide to just take it easy. We kept building sales by providing great service to our precious clients. By the end of that year, we were billing around $60,000 a week for a second-year gross revenue total of $2.9 million.

Fast-forward a few years, and our staffing-services line really took off. We secured a $420,000 staffing contract when that organization's leaders realized the facility needed more help in 2015.

I had a bit of an advantage over our rivals when the request for proposals (RFP) came out for this public agency. I had responded to many large public RFPs at the engineering firm prior to Bright-Star Care, so I knew how to put one together that showed our strengths. In addition, we were already providing similar skilled staffing services for a school in Glen Ellyn, where we were under a five-year public contract. In the DuPage proposal, when we put down everything on paper about our business services and personnel, section by section, it formed a nice-sized book, and we really looked good! To see so plainly on paper what the business had grown into in those few short years made me very proud of what we had become. The credit lies largely with our staff, both field and office personnel. They simply are so good at what they do. We started servicing the new staffing organization in January 2016 and remain their number one staffing provider.

> To see so plainly on paper what the business had grown into in those few short years made me very proud of what we had become.

What makes some of this unique is that we're a single franchise unit operation. Regardless, our first-year sales record didn't last long. Shortly afterward, a cluster of three other BrightStar Care franchisees, including one in Hawaii, eclipsed our record in rapid succession.

In 2015, based on revenue volume, we were the largest single-unit franchise in the system. Presently, we are roughly number two in the system.

FROM CHIEF SALESMAN TO CFO

As I said earlier, nothing matters until you hit breakeven. But once you do that, you have to start paying more attention to the financial aspects of the business. There's more to running a company of any size than just sales. I came into this as a marketing guy. It's something I knew and something I was good at. At my previous job, as a board member, I would sit at board meetings, but after I made my presentation, I didn't pay a whole lot of attention to the other aspects of the business, such as human resources, operations, insurance, and financials. It did not take long in our new BrightStar Care business for me to lament that I wished I had paid more attention back then. I was wearing many more hats than just the marketing/sales ones, and I needed to become a fast learner or fail. Suddenly, I was operating a $3 million business and seat-of-the-pants wasn't going to cut it anymore.

In any business, you simply must grow with it. Before you hit breakeven, you don't pay a lot of attention to financials. However, dealing with seventy-five to one hundred employees is very different than interacting with the first three or four. There are vexing matters such as unemployment and workers' compensation claims. Then there's the whole matter of regulatory compliance and licensure. I had to come to terms with all of that. I must have been too naive to be overwhelmed. I just sort of plowed through it along the way and received significant help and advice from our BrightStar Care neighboring franchisees and the franchisor support.

From the beginning, I knew I didn't have the competency to deal with clinical matters, so I hired experts. That included my wife, Judy, who was our founding director of nursing. Now I function as the chief financial officer, with all the attendant responsibilities for bringing down costs by implementing good management practices—something I would have been incapable of doing a few years ago.

Early on, I didn't realize how aggressively you need to fight unemployment claims. As a result, our unemployment tax went way up. We have people who file for unemployment even though we had assignments going unfilled. We had offered them shifts, and they had turned the shifts down. Presently, those kinds of claims are easy to fight since the country is virtually at full employment. During the downturn, the state was much more likely to approve a claim. That situation affected profitability for several years.

The whole human resources arena has been a learning experience. Coming out of a mature engineering and construction business where we had a lot of well-meaning employees, we'd be able to offer work and they would accept it. In this health care space, however, the employment relationships are more casual, less permanent. We can't make someone take a per diem assignment if they don't want to work the shift. Sometimes they just take the whole week off. It can be very frustrating because the care needs are still there, irrespective of whether we are able to fill the work. Many employees only want to accept ten to fifteen hours a week when we could employ them for forty hours. There also seems to be less employee loyalty to our company, with many signing on with several agencies so they can pick and choose when and where they will work for the week. It is challenging to operate a large-volume health care operation with such a casually minded workforce.

We have roughly 4,800 hours of work per week available and about 275 employees. That averages out to 17.5 hours a week worked per employee. This requires us to carry twice the number of employees needed than if everyone worked full time. We have the work for them. Fortunately, the more advanced staff, such as our high-skilled nurses, tend to have a more professional outlook for their positions and careers.

I don't handle human resources any longer. Our organizational structure is such that there are several layers of capable management at our company that handle most HR matters, including a full-time recruitment specialist. But the main issue of an acute labor shortage in the health care space is not going to go away any time soon. Industry reports indicate that by 2025, the shortage of direct-care workers (caregivers and CNAs) will exceed 550,000.[4] Their total number will exceed those working in the retail industry, making them members of the largest segment of the workforce. The problem with keeping people involved in direct care is salary. There are just too many better-paying jobs out there, and the middle class can't afford much more than it's already doing (in paying for our services).[5]

A strong reason for the gap between need and supply is of course the aging of the baby boomer population.[6] We've been more successful at recruiting employees than some of our peers because we have very sophisticated recruiting systems in place. We're in a favorable spot because of the amount of work we have available for potential employees to pick up. Some of our health care peers tell us they lose employees to us because we have a lot of work available—and yet we're losing work daily because we don't have enough people to fill all the shifts that are placed with us.

---

4   Kelly Gooch, "Analysis: US Projected to Face Shortages of These 6 Healthcare Occupations by 2025," *Becker's Hospital Review*, May 3, 2018, https://www.beckershospitalreview.com/workforce/analysis-us-projected-to-face-shortages-of-these-6-healthcare-occupations-by-2025.html.

5   "PHI Facts," Paraprofessional Healthcare Institute, November 2013, https://phinational.org/wp-content/uploads/legacy/phi-facts-3.pdf.

6   "The Aging Workforce: Challenges for the Health Care Industry Workforce," the NTAR Leadership Center, March 2013, https://www.dol.gov/odep/pdf/NTAR-AgingWorkforceHealthCare.pdf.

We currently have 260 active employees (the number has been as high as 320). Of the 260, 12 are administrators, and 2 are nurse managers. Among the field staff, roughly 110 are CNAs, 90 are caregivers, and the remaining 55 are nurses.

The big transformational growth for me personally came in the area of financials—and surprise, surprise, I found I had the acumen and interest to do true financial management. This was something I ignored when I sat on TSC's board. But if you're going to run a $6.5 million business, you'd better get a handle on it if you want to survive. BrightStar Care provided the basic training, but the rest entailed on-the-job learning. The company's proprietary software system (money well spent, by the way) covers most aspects of the business, coupled with operations manuals and ongoing support. I didn't stray from the system. Now I'm capable of looking at a problem and devising a managerial function that will produce a positive financial outcome. I didn't know any of that at first, but you can only grow as your capacity will allow you. You have to grow your capacity as you go on in life.

I also had to become an expert in insurance and risk management, another area I had ignored in my previous business life in the construction industry, although I understood the risks were high. But even though the risks are much lower in caregiving, they're still there. I learned quickly about workers' compensation insurance and the inevitable claims. The matters of business get serious when one considers that an employee could be seriously, or maybe permanently, injured as a result of simply working for our company. Good workers' comp insurance needs to be in place and the claims managed effectively.

Better yet, we try to have practices in place to avoid injuries. The predominant injuries in caregiving services are back injuries and sprains from lifting patients and transferring patients. Repositioning an overweight patient who is bedridden is not only difficult for the caregiver but risky for an injury. Nurses also risk injuries while on the job. A biggie is the occasional needlestick from an injection. Also, as soon as winter comes along, slips and falls on ice are a problem.

Between the insurance requirements our licenses call for and the coverages BrightStar Care helps us obtain, we are well covered. We also purchase umbrella coverage to make sure we're sort of overprotected. One big claim, and you can imperil the business. You ignore the insurance issue at your own peril.

As I grew into my role as leader, we also added other roles and really built out a multilayered organizational structure. Today, that structure has made it possible for Judy and I to enjoy life in a way that we never imagined when we began BrightStar Care.

CHAPTER 4

Running the Business and Available Services

Have computer and telephone, will travel. In this day and age, there's little reason to be on-site day in and day out to own and manage a business. Judy and I made the leap in 2014 when she retired, moving from Wheaton to Beaufort, South Carolina, which is near Hilton Head Island, and we've never looked back. I manage a $6.5 million business from 963 miles away, and it hums along. The key is to have the right management structure and the right people in those positions. We do.

When we initially put our Wheaton home up for sale, we figured we'd have the better part of a year to prepare for the move. We were wrong. We put the house up for sale January 1, and it sold in twenty-eight days. We closed on March 25, 2014 and had to vacate. That meant moving up our timetable drastically. It was a good thing we already had our key people in place—even if they weren't quite ready for the responsibility. Luckily, they grew into their jobs rapidly.

BRIGHTSTAR CARE OF CENTRAL DUPAGE-WHEATON ACCOUNTABILITY CHART

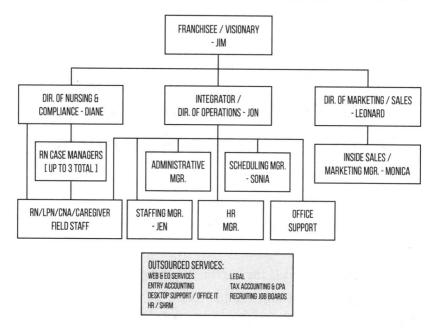

JDF Services Inc., d.b.a. BrightStar Care of Central DuPage–Wheaton, is run according to the Traction Entrepreneurial Operating System by Gino Wickman. It has six tenets: vision, people, issues, data, process, and traction.[7] Once the first five tenets are properly administered, you gain traction so the whole is greater than the sum of its parts. You need accountability—accountability to your company, to yourself, your position, your peers/subordinates, your superiors. So instead of referring to it as an organizational chart, it's called our accountability chart.

After my position, which involves mainly financial management, there are four key areas for BrightStar Care Central DuPage–

---

7   Gino Wickman, *Traction: Get a Grip on Your Business* (Dallas, TX: BenBella Books Inc., 2011).

Wheaton: operations, marketing/sales, clinical caregiving, and clinical compliance. Please note: we emphasize clinical service and excellence to the point that it occupies two of our four executive positions and departments. Our executive-team salary structure is high, and we give generous bonuses as well.

In addition, our key executive team members have been encouraged in the past three years to buy stock in the company at a subsidized price, both as a means of giving them a stake in our success and with an eye toward future ownership once I decide to exit the business. They're all about a decade younger than I am. After I started doing this, my accountant noticed and approved. The goal is to have my executive team own 10 percent of the company in the near future. The ownership transition will continue from there.

When we first moved to South Carolina, I was making monthly, sometimes weekly, trips back to Wheaton. I did that for about two years, but now I think quarterly visits are sufficient. When I am in town, we schedule off-site Traction planning update meetings: two days in January to go over our goals and activities and then one-day meetings in each of the other quarters to refresh those goals. I generally just manage my executive team (Jonathan Gray, director of operations; Kelly Honn, director of nursing; Diane Thorson, director of clinical compliance; and Leonard Sanchez, director of marketing and sales) and leave it to them to manage their reports. The accountability chart conveys clear lines of responsibility, and meeting those levels of responsibility creates the "traction" of a successful organization.

The company has been blessed to have competent, loyal, long-term employees. I could not manage from South Carolina without them.

From there, we are not an extremely structured organization. We always put the client first. None of our care decisions are made on a financial basis. Care decisions are made with compassion and expertise.

We take a comprehensive approach to caring for an individual based on his or her personal and medical conditions, personality, lifestyle, and home environment, providing a higher standard of care in the marketplace.

> Care decisions are made with compassion and expertise.

DIRECTOR OF OPERATIONS

Jonathan Gray and his wife, Sutherland, were our next-door neighbors in Wheaton. For years I watched him get up at 2:30 a.m. to head into Chicago to manage a specialty meat-processing plant for an absentee owner. Then in 2011, there was a change at his company, and he was no longer with them. He needed a job. And though I knew we didn't really need a director of operations at the beginning of 2012 since I was doing that job, I also knew we wanted to move down south and would need someone in the not-too-distant future to take over the day-to-day tasks.

Gray, a father of two and now a grandfather, was really a good fit for the task. He started his working life in sales, and so he knows the importance of that end of the business. More than that, he can empathize with our clients and caregivers since he and his wife provided the bulk of the caregiving for her parents. Also, he is now dealing with those very same issues when it comes to his parents, whom he moved back to Chicago from Florida so he and his sister could handle their care needs. He truly understands that people are entrusting their lives to us. We need to provide dignity and empathy while providing the best possible care.

Gray manages and oversees the entire operational side of the business, including the establishment of new accounts in the system, the servicing of those accounts, scheduling, and order fulfillment. If there's a private-duty shift ordered, it needs to be filled. No exceptions. He supervises billing, payroll, office functions, and human resources.

There is a lot of client and employee churn. That's just the nature of a health care business. Clients are discharged for the most part because they've passed away, run into financial pressures, or gotten better. Employees leave for a variety of reasons, including furthering their education, career advancement, and better-paying opportunities. So Gray also oversees a massive hiring machine. We are perpetually hunting for great employees to serve our clients. With my being gone, he has the toughest job in the company and puts in the most hours. When he first started, he would get into the office at least an hour before anyone else simply because he was so used to getting up at 2:30 a.m.!

In 2014, we were the largest-volume single-unit BrightStar Care agency in the system. That means Jonathan has been operating one of the largest BrightStar Care agencies for some time now. If an issue with a patient is financial or service oriented, Gray is responsible; if the issue falls on the clinical side, that becomes the responsibility of our clinical managers.

DIRECTOR OF MARKETING AND SALES

Our sales/marketing department has a large number of initiatives, including a newsletter, direct mail, local website / SEO, email marketing, inside sales/lead follow-through, social media, and direct sales. Our marketing and sales people include Leonard Sanchez and a dedicated full-time marketing manager.

Sanchez has been on board since July 2009, when I hired him to help with the sales calls as I got more involved in the operations. After me, he is our longest-tenured office employee. Today he is responsible for all marketing and servicing our staffing contracts and makes a minimum of thirty sales calls a week.

Sanchez actually was responsible for our initial involvement in school nursing staffing while cold-calling on West Chicago High School, his alma mater. He hadn't been back there since graduating but decided it was worth paying a call to let the school know about our services. While "taking a walk down memory lane," he was talking with one of the assistant principals when the subject of one-on-one nursing for special-needs students came up, and he let the administrator know we are medically licensed and could provide a nurse on demand.

A short time later, we got a call from the school. One of its nurses had been calling in sick for more than a week, forcing the student she cared for to stay home, and the school was concerned about the great imposition this placed on the student's family. We told them we could have a nurse there the next day. Sanchez ran over with a contract and signed them up, and once they realized the quality of service we could provide, it was a downhill run.

In 2017, we hired a full-time marketing manager who specializes in online and digital marketing, social media, and other aspects of marketing outreach. She is also responsible for following up on the average thirteen to fifteen inquiries that come in weekly. We have a certain message to get out and a high level of engagement that comes from knowing and listening to our audience. She talks to people and can empathize with their unique situations, then looks at our services and pulls all the components together for a personalized proposal—and not just our services but those available throughout the community in general, suggesting such alternatives as adult day care to help bring costs down. It is about understanding what the client is seeking as the end result, then directing him or her to the proper resources to have his or her needs met.

DIRECTOR OF NURSING

Kelly Honn, RN, was one of our first hires. She started as a field nurse but soon was tapped as assistant director of nursing as Judy's caseload expanded. Honn came to nursing as a second career. She was working as a financial adviser when the planes flew into the World Trade Center in New York on September 11, 2001. People stopped investing, and she was out of a job. A neighbor down the street had no family and needed help with such things as going to doctor appointments. That was her first exposure to the world of caregiving and made her realize that she liked taking care of people. Herself a very caring person, she got a sense of fulfilling one of those deep callings in life. There was a shortage of nurses at the time, so Honn went back to school and in 2008 earned her RN.

Honn worked as a field nurse for two years before she was brought in to help Judy and took over as director of nursing when Judy retired in early 2014. She spends the majority of her time with patients and their families. A case generally starts with a family calling for service. There is a living room visit first, generally by a nurse, to assess the situation and learn the client's needs. If we can help, the nurse signs up the client and prepares an assessment to structure a care plan. The case is assigned to a nurse-case manager (we have had as many as four, depending on the number of patients). The director of nursing also acts as one of the case managers. In addition, per our skilled licensure requirements, there is always an RN on call at our agency. This is in addition to the regular on-call at the business.

We manage each case through a digital portal that our CNAs

and field nurses can log in to through their smartphones to determine what is needed. There's also a lot of verbal communication with our caregivers. Employee training / competency levels and availabilities are matched with patient needs.

When we bring field staff on board, their skills are assessed and logged. We require at least one year of experience in the field prior to working with us, and they also go through a thorough competency-training program designed by BrightStar Care to augment their skills and bring them up to the premium level we require.

DIRECTOR OF COMPLIANCE

Early on, we realized we needed someone to keep track of our licenses and certifications so we could remain Illinois Department of Public Health (IDPH) licensed and Joint Commission accredited. Diane Thorson, MSN, makes sure everything is up to date and compliant. Like Judy, she started as a pediatric nurse at what was then Children's Memorial Hospital upon graduation from Valparaiso University. She decided to get her master's from Loyola University so she could get into health care management. Along the way, she did some pediatric home health care and eventually was approached to be director of a home health agency. Again, like Judy, she found her pediatric training translated nicely to geriatric care.

Her decision to move to BrightStar Care from her previous position was fueled in part by her belief that patients and their families should be able to express the care and service needs they require, not Medicare. Along with her duties making sure BrightStar Care remains Joint Commission approved, she acts as a case manager for a number of BrightStar Care clients, making sure their care plans are up to date and that those plans are altered when the need arises.

When an employee is hired, there are at least fifty items that need to be checked off. Issues such as a valid driver's license, tuberculosis testing, biannual CPR certification, and many more preemployment criteria. She also oversees an employee continuing education program consisting of twelve one-hour lessons or continuing education units (CEUs) annually related to each position. This is for nontechnical staff such as caregivers and CNAs. Nurses have a separate program that she monitors.

Since the update to our IDPH licenses occurs annually, the compliance officer also has to keep an eye on the current and next years' licensing requirements, making sure all the necessary information is included in the applications. The compliance officer develops policies and procedures and is responsible for implementing a performance-improvement solution in areas where we have challenges and/or process failures.

WE PUT THE HEART IN HOME CARE

There are two main segments to the business: home care and facilities staffing.

Home Care

Our goal is to reduce the physical difficulty of daily tasks and increase home safety. Home care has three segments and represents about two-thirds of our business volume.

Hourly services are either nonmedical or personal care. Nonmedical services involve assisting clients with basic functions so they can remain safely in their homes. These services include light housekeeping, transportation, meal preparation, and companionship. And though they cannot dispense medication, our caregivers can observe while a client takes it—or doesn't—and report back.

Another segment is personal care, which covers a deeper level of daily living, including help with getting out of bed, toileting, bathing, grooming, ambulation, and well-being checks. Personal care is just a shade under nursing care. Personal care aides can service a catheter bag but cannot give injections or do glucose checks or administer medication, although they can watch and report whether those things are being done. Many of our agency's CNAs are live-ins. Overall, CNAs represent half of our home care business (about a third of the business overall). They not only staff private homes but provide services in assisted living and retirement communities.

> Since live-ins are in the home twenty-four hours a day, sometimes seven days a week, they tend to become part of the family.

Since live-ins are in the home twenty-four hours a day, sometimes seven days a week, they tend to become part of the family. They are the silent heroes of the agency and generally enable a person to stay at a current level of living without having to advance to the next step. A typical live-in's day is twelve hours of work, four hours of personal time and eight hours of sleep.

The third level of home care is skilled care. It's a relatively small part of our business and requires a high level of skilled staff. If a client is a hospice patient, twenty-four-hour nursing may be required. Additional skilled care services involve such things as IV therapy, wound care, various medication administration, injections, ventilator care, or trach-tube care.

They also can administer infusions, obviating the necessity for clients to travel to a doctor's office or hospital for chemotherapy or other medications, which can take three or four hours to administer. Health care statistics have determined that one of the major causes of readmission to the hospital after discharge is the mismanagement of follow-up medication, and our skilled services can help a family avoid a readmission.

Another service we provide for our home care patients is sending a nurse out once a week to make sure their medication boxes are properly filled and instruct the caregiver on monitoring the medication intake.

We're all about health solutions and service. We do the heavy lifting in terms of finding the right caregivers for any given situation. When patients come out of the hospital or rehab, they and their families just don't have the time—or the ability—to do things like check credentials, competencies, and backgrounds.

We also have the ability to craft individual solutions. It's not one size fits all. We start by listening to the needs the patient and his or her family are trying to meet. Maybe it's a couple where the husband has dementia and the wife has been taking care of him, but now she's hospitalized or in rehab. Or maybe a potential client had been getting by with care a few hours a day but now needs someone 24-7 because "Mom just can't be left alone anymore."

We develop a plan based on those individual needs and adjust the plan as those needs change.

Many times, when an individual is discharged from the hospital, the family is overwhelmed by the instructions. Maybe there's confusion about the medication or they have no idea how to arrange for follow-up care. We can provide that support based on our clinical strengths. Though hospitals and rehab centers refer patients to us, we still need to reach out. We use ads on social media to point people to our website. Our portal is set up so that once an email address is supplied, we can send targeted emails explaining our services without overwhelming potential clients.

We also take part in community events like Taste of Wheaton to get our brand out there, and we have a referral campaign. Once a client is signed, we send out a welcome packet (targeted toward the client's adult child) with a five-dollar Starbucks card and information on our team and business practices, like invoicing. In that packet are referral brochures they can pass on to friends with little cards that say, "I recommend BrightStar Care," on which they can put their names. If the referral becomes a new client, we send the referring client a VIP pass for direct contact with one of our nurses.

Some inquiries never go beyond price shopping. We're the premium-priced provider in our marketplace, and as such we are a great fit for clients who understand that is the service level their loved one will be receiving. We just are not a good fit for those who view low price as the main objective. But once one considers our premium-service scope, skilled medical licensing, and Joint Commission accreditation, the value is there in terms of meeting the care needs of the client. We simply provide a higher quality of service. People certainly appreciate what that means when they really need it.

> We just are not a good fit for those who view low price as the main objective.

One challenging part of the job is watching other people struggle. You can hear it in their voices when they call up for the first time and don't even really know what they're asking for. It is a privilege, almost a sacred privilege, when they tell us about the personal needs of their loved one, entrusting us with that information. It's personal, and we treat it as such as we attempt to craft the perfect match.

We do follow-up calls even with those who do not take our services to find out what they did decide. That's information we can use to make our solutions even stronger.

Facilities Staffing

When it comes to providing staff to our medical-facilities clients, we think of ourselves as a medical version of Manpower or Robert Half, the temporary-employment agencies. We do this under an Illinois Department of Labor license as well as the license we have from IDPH. Most BrightStar Care franchises are medically licensed and can do facility staffing. And because we do medical staffing, our other services are conducted on a much higher level than a typical nonmedical agency.

It all started with Sanchez's visit to his old high school. Once we had West Chicago signed up, Sanchez went to every other public school in our territory and the private schools as well. Once they experienced our level of service, we chased all of the other agencies out. We now staff virtually all of the schools in our territory, not just with one-on-one nurses for special-needs students but school nurses as well, representing about $15,000 in weekly billings. If a school decides it wants to hire one of our people full time, it can do so by paying us a fee. (That happens on the live-in side of our business as well. All of our contracts have a provision for direct hire of our staff.)

In late 2009, when a nursing home in our area was short CNAs, they came to us. That's where we got our first experience at facilities staffing. One grew into two and then more. We met a need for facilities that had difficulty hiring nurses and CNAs for most all their shifts. We continue to help there weekly on an as-needed basis so there is enough staff to handle their patient needs. And when the director of nursing at Sunrise of Glen Ellyn went on maternity leave, we filled the gap until her return.

By and large, the bulk of our staffing business is at large health care facilities. They are able to operate effectively with our help. Some weeks, we fill 300 to 350 CNA and nurse staffing shifts. Trying to hire that many additional employees would be cost prohibitive for the facilities. For us, it takes a special subset of staff to fill those shifts, and they work alongside regular employees at the facility. Our staff can be given a whole wing to manage, where they are responsible for the bathing, feeding, and toileting of the residents. Overnight, they can be responsible for up to twelve to twenty patients. Nurses, generally LPNs, are tasked with medical management, wound care, and trach issues, sometimes for an entire floor at the facility. When it comes to medications, they can't make a single mistake, ever, and that is a tremendous responsibility.

Our people staff assisted living facilities, clinics, hospice providers, hospitals, independent-living facilities, medical offices, nursing homes, retirement community centers, schools, rehabilitation centers, home health care agencies, private-duty agencies, special-needs residential schools, on-site wellness and treatment clinics, flu-shot clinics, workers' compensation patients, and long-term-care-insurance patients. The primary positions we staff in our marketplace are RNs, LPNs, CNAs, and caregivers.

Alzheimer's

Alzheimer's is a widespread disease that afflicts a large portion of the senior population. It is the sixth-leading cause of death in the nation, and more than sixteen million Americans provide unpaid care for people with Alzheimer's or other dementias.[8]

This disease provides unique challenges to the senior-care business. Seniors forget to pay their bills, or they get confused. Sometimes

---

8   Alzheimer's Association, "Facts and Figures," accessed June 24, 2019, https://www.alz.org/alzheimers-dementia/facts-figures.

they forget a scheduled service, or they won't open the door for the caregiver. It makes certain functions of the business harder.

As an example of some of the "issues" that can occur helping our memory-care patients, we had a patient with deep memory issues who listed herself as the only contact on the case. She was mixed up on paying her weekly invoices, and the payments had been very erratic. When our office staff contacted her, she hung up on them. So I got involved. At one point, she turned the phone over to her husband, but he also didn't understand the situation, and he eventually hung up on me as well. Since she had given us her email address, I decided to send an email. A family member must have handled the email, which allowed a rational resolution to the problem.

BrightStar Care has a set of specific competencies to help us serve our memory-care patients. For starters, home health aides have a minimum one-year experience, have undergone extensive background and credentials checks, and are trained in the BrightStar Care dementia care approach. Also, an RN oversees every case to supervise the individualized plan of care. We also provide 24-7 live-answer communication and support. And we help to educate family caregivers about what to expect with their loved one's disease.

Transitional Care

The clients in our service area are fortunate. They get premium care at Northwestern Medicine's Central DuPage Hospital and premium follow-up care from us. Together, we are improving the general health of our area. There's a synergy that really benefits our mutual patients.

If a patient is discharged to hospice, we provide compassionate care, and our staff has specialized end-of-life training and will coordinate with the main hospice team.

Child Care

A very small segment of our business involves child care. This is the result of national BrightStar Care contracts that provide the service as part of employee-benefit contracts. The service enables a company employee to obtain emergency child care if a child gets sick or a regular nanny or babysitter doesn't show up, enabling that parent to go to work.

WHAT WE DON'T HANDLE

BrightStar Care Central DuPage–Wheaton does not provide speech, occupational, or physical therapists, nor do we provide the main Medicare-paid home health services. We simply do not hire personnel such as physical therapists and the like. There are so many great physical therapy clinics in our area, that it does not make sense for us to get involved in this space of the market. Central DuPage Hospital alone has twenty off-site clinics. We would rather drive one of our clients to one of these clinics than attempt to provide the service ourselves.

CHAPTER 5

It's All about People

One of the best things about being involved in the caregiving business is the people you meet on both sides of the equation, the clients and our great employees. As I've said before, it takes a really special person to dedicate his or her talents to the well-being of others. We still have some caregivers who have been with us from the beginning. They truly are selfless!

On the other side are our clients, who are all unique and special. One man especially came from a truly remarkable family. He was a renowned architect, well known for his design work on homes and public buildings. He was active in his community, very involved in local community affairs. He lived alone quite well with his three cats. Then, one day, he fell. We met with his family at Lake Forest Hospital because that's where his family doctor had privileges. He didn't want to go into rehab. He and his family wanted him to go back to the place he loved best, his home. His son and daughter decided to hire us, and we started by providing twenty-four-hour nursing care to meet his posthospital needs. When he improved, we switched the care to double live-ins. Judy was constantly on call for him and would race over whenever the need arose. He never did walk again but managed to get around the house on a scooter. At one point, he fell into a coma, and everyone was convinced that was it. I remember Judy coming back from a visit in the home. She was so upset, she sat down at our kitchen table and cried. The whole family gathered around his bed. While his granddaughter was stroking his hand, he woke up and very lucidly asked what they were all doing there. The startled family quickly covered by telling him that they were just there visiting. Unfortunately, that event was the beginning of the end, and shortly after that he passed away.

> We still have some caregivers who have been with us from the beginning. They truly are selfless!

I went over to visit one time, just to say hello. He was sitting in his scooter with a stack of mail in front of him and turned to me and asked, "You know how I decide what mail to open? I sniff it. If it's perfumed, I open it. Otherwise, it goes into the trash." His wife had died a number of years earlier. They had had a successful life and marriage, even though she had contracted polio shortly after their wedding and was wheelchair bound. In addition to being an architect, he was an accomplished artist. Our family even has reprints of some of his watercolors hanging around our house and in my home office. Most of the pictures were done as he and his wife traveled. She would give him a half a day to do one of his paintings while she did something else. Many of the paintings became their family Christmas cards for that year's travels.

In a stark example about the outcomes of our care, at the funeral home, his children came up to Judy and thanked her for giving them an extra three and a half years with their father.

A few years ago, one of our star caregivers, Dawn Wilson, literally saved a client's life just by being observant and knowing her charge. She is one of our short-shift employees, meaning she spends a few hours a day with several clients. This particular gentleman she saw for two hours or so every afternoon to help with his bathing, hygiene care, toileting, and laundry and other chores. He used both a wheelchair and walker and was diabetic and a fall risk. She'd remind him about his medications, but he took his own insulin shots.

One afternoon, she noticed he seemed a bit off. He was slurring his words, and since diabetes put him at risk of a stroke, she contacted our nurse manager. The nurse rushed over, and, despite his protests that he was fine, she called other family members and notified 911 to send an ambulance. At the emergency room, he was diagnosed as having a stroke, and the doctor told us he had gotten to the ER in the nick of time. His family was beyond grateful. We got a call the next day thanking us for being so observant, catching the signs, and acting on them.

That man remained a client of ours through February 2017, about eight months after the stroke. At that time, he moved into assisted living because his wife had suddenly died. She had been his main caregiver, and after her passing he simply could not remain home alone.

More recently, one of our CNAs took care of an elderly woman suffering from cancer. Her daughters had been handling her needs but were exhausted. They wanted a CNA to live in and take care of her, ferrying her to and from doctors' appointments and chemotherapy.

We assigned Novelita "Novie" Marzalado, who had been a CNA since 2011. She cared for the woman for just three weeks before she died, but her family was so grateful, they sent us a glowing letter:

> Dear BrightStar: I am writing this to thank you and especially Novie for being there for my mother.
>
> Novie took great care of my Mom … for most of July 2018. She was so attentive, with great attitude and cheer. We laughed a lot considering the challenges. Mom was happy with her even if she preferred her daughters giving all of her care. Novie was much more skilled than we were.

Novie went above and beyond in her care of Mom. She anticipated her needs and helped us with ours as well. She was always there in the day and night. She kept up with all the laundry, dishes, food. She cleaned the cupboards and labeled the expiration dates on the items. We were thrilled and amazed.

It was an extra tough job because the house was always full of people coming and going, cooking and messing it up. She helped with that as well. Not an easy job.

We were so thankful for her. I saw a form that I didn't manage to keep from your company. It was to recommend a great caretaker for an award.

Novie deserves that and the best heartfelt thank you from myself and the rest of the … family.

Thanks again for sending us Novie.

The letter was signed by one of the woman's daughters.

I'll share one more patient story. This one involves a current client who is very exacting in her demands. When she gives a compliment, we take notice. We provide her with help two hours a day, seven days a week, because she wants to maintain the highest level of independence as possible. She is at risk of falls and pressure sores and uses a walker and wheelchair. We help her with showering, oversee her dressing, do light cleaning and laundry, cook meals, and assist with personal-care needs. We encourage her to do her range-of-motion exercises. We try to keep her safe from falls, infections, and hospitalizations.

So when she nominated our CNA Elisa Ballines for employee of the month, we were pleased. This note was sent to Jonathan Gray, our director of operations.

Dear Mr. Gray,

I'm not certain how BrightStar recognizes their employees, but I would like to nominate Elisa B. as Employee of the Month. I recently took your survey and realized that I should share my appreciation directly with your office.

I based my caregiver questions on Elisa as she is with me an average of four days a week while the remaining women each only come once a week.

Elisa has been with me since January and has never disappointed me. Her professional presentation is only the beginning of her assets. She is reliable, knowledgeable, conscientious, attentive, empathetic and cheerful. She was thoughtful enough to bring me flowers on my birthday, and she has given me a shoulder to cry on when I've had an emotional day. She treats me as a friend rather than another client, which I really appreciate. In short, she does an outstanding job of fulfilling my needs. She also takes exceptional care of my equipment, which is a bonus. I always look forward to seeing her, knowing that I will be taken care of in a consistent fashion.

I hope you will share this information with Diane [Thorson, compliance director] and consider acknowledging Elisa. She takes great pride in her job, and I am certain she would welcome recognition of her efforts with your organization.

Relationships like these do not develop by accident. They grow out of our philosophy toward not just premium caregiving but life in general.

As mentioned earlier, I went to divinity school and try to incorporate spirituality into every aspect of my life. At the end of the day, I want to be proud of what I've accomplished. I tend to set high goals for myself and those around me. It's OK if that goal isn't met immediately. What's important is striving for it and learning from one's inability to meet it. It goes beyond the power of positive thinking, but if you know what you want in life or in business and continually work toward it, you can achieve it. Take our first-year sales record. I and our entire office staff were engaged in the same vision. We didn't give up, and by the end of the first year, we had achieved our goal.

> Relationships like these do not develop by accident. They grow out of our philosophy toward not just premium caregiving but life in general.

PATIENT ASSESSMENTS

Managing a client's needs starts with a home visit by one of our RNs, who first talks with the family about the services they may need and the costs. We determine the kinds of things a client can and cannot do for themselves as well as how much family members can and cannot handle. The assessments begin with "Tell me what's going on" so we can get an idea of what kinds of things they need us to do for their loved one.

We have a template for the assessment, which measures such things as alertness, orientation, and pain levels. It's a typical nursing assessment, much like what you would undergo in a hospital setting. Can the client walk unassisted or does he or she need someone for support? Is there a fall risk? Is he or she bedridden? What self-care can he or she perform on his or her own? Can he or she manage his or her own medication? It also looks at home safety, such as whether there are grab bars in the shower or trip hazards around the house. The assessment helps us determine whether the client needs a caregiver, a CNA, or a nurse for skilled nursing.

Our CNAs are certified to handle Foley catheters, take vital signs, and turn and reposition patients. They do not dose and/or administer medication but observe whether medications are being taken properly at the right time. They watch whether diabetic patients are monitoring their sugar levels properly and taking the right amount of insulin. If not, one of our nurses is summoned to reevaluate the situation. We rely on daily staff notes to determine whether a situation is in flux and if changes need to be made to the care plan.

Sometimes our initial assessment determines that a client needs a lot more care than the family anticipated.

CONTINUING EDUCATION UNITS

As part of our IDPH licensure and Joint Commission accreditation, we require our caregivers and CNAs to take twelve hours of ongoing training every year in the form of CEUs. We used to tell them to read a chapter and then take a test on paper. But in 2017, we instituted an online version. Our people watch a webinar and then take a test online. We can pull up the results immediately—and so can the Joint Commission. We call it "In the Know."

A different subject is presented every month. In 2017–18, the topics included the following:

- Maintaining confidentiality
- Protecting clients during flu season
- Disaster planning
- Understanding abuse and neglect
- Home care safety tips
- Understanding fall-risk factors
- Oxygen safety for CNAs
- Safe environments for clients with dementia and Alzheimer's disease
- Building trust and confidence with clients
- Discovering your flair for excellent client care
- Client-centered care
- Handling incontinence and UTIs

The first four topics selected for 2018–19 were the patient bill of rights, standard precautions, activities for clients with Alzheimer's disease, and understanding abuse and neglect. Each year, we require the first block of topics to be completed by March 1, the second by July 1, and the third by November 1.

Nurses also are required to take twenty hours of continuing education by the Illinois Department of Financial and Professional Regulation over a two-year period. There's no specific regimen provided by the state, so nurses have to get those hours on their own.

Our director of compliance makes sure our people complete the work, but each staffer is responsible for getting it done.

The topics are chosen from a list of seventy-three provided by the state of Illinois. Among the other topics are understanding the normal aging process, understanding autism, taking care of your back, the CNA/nurse relationship, and understanding common medications.

We rotate topics every year to make sure our people have a diverse, all-around understanding of the issues related to their positions and placement in the homes.

Every July, we also call all active staff members into the office for an hour to talk about some of our quality control issues. Things we track and issues that we monitor for include falls, handwashing, and complaints. We also usually roll out something new (such as the online education modules), and we do performance reviews and credential checks and go over client compliments.

In 2017, I was happy to report to the team that IDPH's on-site survey that year had found no deficiencies in our operation. The previous year, we had forgotten to print out something and put it into a file folder, hence a ding! We learned our lesson and corrected that matter ASAP!

FINDING THE RIGHT PEOPLE

> The BrightStar Care brand is "A Higher Standard of Care," and we hold our people to that higher standard.

Our BrightStar Care franchise system has excellent hiring practices in place that include a very robust recruitment regimen. Our people must have at least one year of experience to qualify because they largely work on their own, without a supervisor constantly looking over their shoulders. It raises the quality metric a bit.

The BrightStar Care brand is "A Higher Standard of Care," and we hold our people to that higher standard. We make sure they have the resolve to serve with passion and go in with a positive outlook—

no matter what's going on in their personal lives. We also always let them know when they've done something really well. Our people work hard, and when they go home, they can feel good about what they've done that day.

Our caregivers prefer to either work in individual homes, where there's more of a one-on-one personal relationship with the client, or on the medical-staffing side, where it's more about working for a facility. Although the care provided is very similar, there is little crossover between the two types of roles. Generally, on the one-on-one side, the hours vary from just an hour a day in a given home to twelve-hour shifts. Our one-on-one caregivers may have four or five clients a day, but they put their entire focus on one patient at a time. On the staffing side, the rule is generally eight-hour shifts, with the caregiver handling multiple patients. Those who work in facilities must be energetic since they're taking care of numerous patients.

All of our people have to be good at accepting direction not only from superiors but also from the patient and family members.

It's tough for our office to keep up with the demand, especially in the area of recruiting and scheduling. If there's a need for caregivers and CNAs, we post jobs on all the major job boards and aggressively pursue candidates. It seems as soon as we have just about enough staff on board, then suddenly demand drops, and we have the risk of our people leaving because their hours fall off. The same thing happens with RNs and LPNs. It's a vicious cycle that keeps us on our toes constantly. Ultimately, we never seem to hire enough staff, so we are constantly recruiting and hiring.

At any given time, we could use about twenty more nurses and fifty to sixty more CNAs. But there's an overall health-care-worker shortage in our society, and it continues to worsen. We leave a minimum of at least 120 hours of staffing work unfilled each week, which is the equivalent of three full-time positions. Accordingly, if we were fully staffed, our clients would be ordering a lot more work from us that presently we do not even see. As it is, our clients on the staffing side know we can cover only so much of their needs (they have the same manpower shortage as us), which forces them to pay overtime and bonuses in order to get their full-time staff to put in more time to meet their needs. The healthcare worker shortage is hurting our growth.

Still, our recruiter always has a smile on her face. She was a CNA before she got into the human resources side of the business. She grew up helping her mother care for her older sister, who suffered from cerebral palsy. Helping her mother made her want to do the same thing for others and make a difference in other people's lives. But she learned very quickly that caring for strangers is different than caring for a loved one.

Six hours into her first job, she realized the hiring practices at the facility where she was working needed help. Some of the CNAs with whom she was working would leave patients and their care needs unattended. It was inhumane. She sought out the administrator and told her she thought changes in their hiring practices needed to be made. Within a year, she was sitting in the human resources chair.

At a time when workers don't place a lot of stock in company loyalty, our recruiter helps us find home caregivers who work for us for the fulfillment. Yes, they want to get paid, but it's not just about the salary. They could get full-time jobs at any number of facilities, but they want the engagement and satisfaction that comes from making a difference in the lives of their clients. That fulfillment and personal bonding is critical, not just with the client but with the client's family. Their loyalty is remarkable.

Secondarily, training is important to them. They're interested in what their employer can give to them in the way of ongoing professional education and development, so they appreciate our CEU program.

Since our five core values are the basis of why and how we do business, we want caregivers who exhibit those values. During the interview process, we ask potential hires why they want to work in health care. If they say that's where the money's at, we are suspect in hiring them. We're looking for people who have a true caring or caregiving nature. We examine whether they've had longevity in their past positions or whether they're job hoppers. We ask why they left a previous position and why it will be different this time.

Asking about previous positions helps us identify potential problems with certain roles or why they might actually be a good fit. For instance, when interviewing for an overnight caregiver, we found one applicant who had been in the role with another employer but had been let go because she couldn't seem to stay awake. She had all the right qualifications for a day job, but we had to look further to fill the overnight role. Another applicant gave all the right answers to our questions. She was almost too perfect, which made our recruiter suspicious. The candidate was cagey when our recruiter tried to get her to open up about her personal life. So a second interviewer was asked to join them and got the candidate to explain that she was recently divorced following a fifteen-year marriage and working multiple jobs to try to make ends meet so she could take care of her children, one of whom had special needs. She was considering putting her son into a home because she just couldn't afford to take care of him herself anymore. We hired her and brought her in for orientation, one of eight people invited to take part. Of the eight, she was one of three who showed up. At the end of orientation at 5:00 p.m., she accepted several shifts, one of which was an overnight shift that began at 7:00

p.m. that evening, which meant she had to find a babysitter for her children. She has become one of our best caregivers ever.

We encourage all of our caregivers to go back to school and get their CNA certifications or to nursing school so that their career advancement and earning power is not limited.

LAWS OF SUCCESS

In his book Think and Grow Rich, Napoleon Hill studied the most successful people of his age in a quest to learn and teach just why they had such great achievements. He looked at people like Henry Ford, Thomas Edison, John Rockefeller, Andrew Carnegie, and many other icons. Among the many commonalities he found were seventeen "success principles." The first of the principles that each and every one of them had was a "chief aim, a definite purpose," one overriding identified goal that they set out to achieve. Hill advises writing that purpose down, which I did before we ever opened.

> ### MY CHIEF AIM DESIRE
>
> By March 9, 2012 our BrightStar business will bill 5,000 hours per week. In return I will gladly provide 85-100 hours per week of efficient service, focusing a majority of that time on Marketing, Sales & Customer Service.
>
> I believe I have this goal in my possession. My faith is so strong I can now see it before my eyes, touch it with my hands and understand it is awaiting transfer to me in proportion to the service I render to others.

Here's my version. I keep it under the glass on my desk.

I set a goal (Hill's definite purpose) of servicing and billing five thousand hours a week by March 9, 2012. It didn't happen by that date, but we kept working toward it. By the third quarter of 2016, it was a reality. Yes, it came almost four and one-half years later than the original time line, but we achieved it. There is something about writing down what you want from life. Somehow writing it down puts you on the path to it actually working out. At the time, that meant about $100,000 in billings a week. We're passed that revenue figure now. It goes back to Emerson's essay on "Compensation." I had made a deal with myself. To reach that five-thousand-hour goal, I promised to provide eighty-five to one hundred hours a week of marketing. You indeed do reap what you sow!

Another one of Hill's seventeen attributes he found in successful people is the concept of the "mastermind." This involves two or more people coming together in a spirit of harmony, and with a definite purpose, they create something that is greater than the sum of the parts. The collaboration allows new ideas to blossom, forming a creative energy that helps them to move forward.

> There is something about writing down what you want from life. Somehow writing it down puts you on the path to it actually working out.

Hill also advises forming a posse—a group of like-minded people dedicated to achieving success—and suggests meeting with the group regularly, either in person or by phone, to talk about any situations and come up with ideas for resolving them.

Self-confidence and control are key as well. And you always need to provide more service than you are paid to do. Accurate thinking also is a major component: you can't be squishy or relativistic. When it comes to success, everything is black and white. When I call staff members, they know they have to have definitive answers. Facts matter. Deadlines have to be set and met. Our office team has admitted they have become more accurate in their thinking as a result of this emphasis in our business.

Another key to success is the Golden Rule. Every day, I really do think about how I want to be treated and how I then treat everyone else. One day, I bought a soft drink at a gas station. I gave the clerk twenty dollars, but the cash drawer didn't have any singles. So the clerk went into the next register, got confused, and gave me five dollars too much in change. When I pointed it out to the cashier, the guy behind me said that if I did not want the extra five dollars, I should have paid his bill! The clerk, however, thanked me profusely. I told her we all have to live with ourselves. Our business is conducted with the same principles.

Most mornings, I take a half hour for what I call daily devotions, about as long as it takes to drink a piping-hot cup of coffee. My devotions are designed to give me a personal connection with God for the purpose of spiritual growth. And while nobody would character-ize me as overly prayerful, I have been reading my theological texts from grad school days and also read A Spiritual Clinic, by J. Oswald Sanders, which contains nineteen lessons tied to scripture and prayer.

Lately, I've been thinking about King David and all that he accomplished. He was far from perfect and admits to such in the Psalms. I also identify with the biblical heroes Caleb and Joshua, two of the twelve spies Moses sent into the promised land to report back on conditions. They were the only members of the group who had that positive vision of what could be. Because the others didn't and the rest of the people were fearful, they along with Moses were condemned to wander the desert for forty more years until all the naysayers had died. If our perspective is right, these historical examples can teach us a lot about how to live in our modern day.

> Handled correctly, with changed behavior as the result, you can grow so much from disappointments and failure.

Learning from failure is important. I learn more from conflict and negative circumstances and mistakes than I do from general victories.

Victories can be taken for granted and lead to easy coasting in life. When you fail, you are forced to concentrate, thinking about what you could have done differently, like whether you made the wrong hire or wasted money on something you shouldn't have bought. It's a problem-solving experience. Handled correctly, with changed behavior as the result, you can grow so much from disappointments and failure.

It is said that "success leaves clues." There is great success all around us, but how often do we observe and follow up on the clues? I talk about this stuff in our leadership meetings and try to leave my staff clues on a continuing basis. As an example, I tell them, "You know how much the company is worth. Find a way to buy me out." Implicit in this is they, too, can enjoy the success Judy and I have earned by doing such.

WHY CLIENTS CHOOSE BRIGHTSTAR CARE CENTRAL DUPAGE-WHEATON

There's a natural selection process in how clients come to us because we are private pay.

I have always said about this business "that we see the best in families" when their loved one has care needs or major health issues. There's a team effort among siblings and sometimes a spouse. They are fierce defenders of their loved one in terms of health care and well-being. We become the go-to agency because of our extensive services and medical licensure. Our executive team is composed of two businesspeople and two clinicians, but the care decisions are made solely on the clinical side. It's a healthy way to run things.

CHAPTER 6

The Stay-at-Home Option

Medicare and health insurance payers provide home health care services only under a doctor's orders and only for certain things, like post-op procedures, intermittent blood draws, physical therapy, speech pathology, and occupational therapy—things that need to be done by a skilled provider—for various lengths of time, typically in the range of three weeks or less. Such services need to be provided by a Medicare-approved agency. But if the required services are more than intermittent, Medicare will not pick up the tab. People qualify for Medicare-paid services if they have trouble leaving their homes without the help of a cane, wheelchair, walker, or other device because of illness or injury.[9]

Beyond the three weeks, which in some cases can be extended for a short period of time, or for what Medicare defines as custodial care, the patient and the patient's family are responsible for picking up the tab. And don't look to Medigap policies to cover those costs. Supplement insurance plans take their cues from Medicare, meaning they generally don't cover what Medicare doesn't cover.

Home health agencies coordinate their services with a doctor's

---

9   "Medicare & Home Health Care," Center for Medicare and Medicaid Services, accessed July 10, 2019, https://www.medicare.gov/Pubs/pdf/10969-Medicare-and-Home-Health-Care.pdf.

orders. If covered, the services tend to cost the patient little or nothing at all. If any durable medical equipment is necessary, the patient is responsible for up to 20 percent of the cost.[10]

Medicare covers a lot, but many patients need more: live-in help to prepare meals and aid in bathing, dressing, and using the bathroom as well as cleaning and laundry. There is legislation that allows Medicare Advantage plans to pay for certain custodial care services, but the hours of care are expected to be less than forty hours per year and are more to cover respite instead of ongoing care.

BrightStar Care is here to fill the gap in the limited services Medicare may pay for and what the family actually needs. But it comes at a cost, as these services are privately paid for. Long-term-care plans also will pay for these services.

LONG-TERM-CARE INSURANCE

Such costs can quickly eat up one's life savings. And though Medicaid will cover costs for the truly indigent, long-term-care insurance may be the best option for the middle class.

Long-term-care insurance companies are expected to pay out $100 billion in the next decade, the American Association for Long-Term Care Insurance estimates. In 2017, claims totaled $9.2 billion, with nearly three-quarters for individuals age eighty and older.[11] The trick, however, is to buy the insurance before age, chronic diseases, and conditions begin taking a toll on one's health. Judy and I are somewhat emphatic with our baby boomer peers that purchasing long-term-care

---

10   "Your Medicare Coverage," Medicare.gov, accessed July 10, 2019, https://www. medicare.gov/coverage/home-health-services.html.

11   Jesse Slome, "Long-Term Care Insurance Companies Will Pay Out $100 Billion over Next Decade," *American Association for Long-Term Care Insurance*, July 10, 2018, https://www.expertclick.com/NewsRelease/LongTerm-Care-Insurance-Companies-Will-Pay-Out-100-Billion-Over-Next-Decade-American-Associat,2018159539.aspx.

insurance is so necessary as part of overall financial planning.

AARP estimates more than half of those sixty-five years of age today will need long-term care at some point in their later years, but financial advisers say it's difficult to convince clients they should buy the insurance—even high-net-worth clients with assets exceeding $1 million.[12] It's a tough conversation. No one wants to acknowledge the day may come when help will be needed for day-to-day tasks, which AARP says will likely average $140,000 out of pocket.[13] And with fewer insurance companies offering such insurance, qualifying for policies is getting more difficult. Large companies in the long-term-care-insurance field, such as Prudential, Metropolitan Life, John Hancock, and Unum, are not underwriting new policies, although they are still servicing those purchased earlier.

> AARP estimates more than half of those sixty-five years of age today will need long-term care at some point in their later years.

AARP advises people to start looking for long-term-care policies no later than their fifties and early sixties.[14] Currently, only 7.2 million Americans have long-term-care coverage to cover expenses not covered by Medicare.

Traditional long-term-care policy costs vary significantly, but expect to pay $1,500 to $3,500 per year depending on your situation.

---

12   Carmen Reinicke, "If You're in Your 50s, You need to Plan for Long-Term Care Right Now," *CNBC*, June 22, 2018, https://www.cnbc.com/2018/06/22/if-youre-in-your-50s-you-need-to-plan-for-long-term-care-right-now.html.

13   Ellen Stark, "5 Things You Should Know about Long-Term Care Insurance," *AARP*, March 1, 2018, https://www.aarp.org/caregiving/financial-legal/info-2018/long-term-care-insurance-fd.html.

14   Ibid.

In exchange, should you require long-term care, the policy pays a specific daily benefit amount based on what you purchased in your policy. Typical daily benefit rates range from $100 to $400 per day. The higher the daily amount, the higher your initial premiums will be. This daily benefit amount is typically raised at the rate of inflation, something else that is built into the policies.

You must qualify for the start of benefits payments based on a medical assessment as to the extent of your care needs. If approved by the carrier, your daily benefits begin. After the insured qualifies for benefits, there is typically an initial waiting period of zero to one hundred days. No benefits are paid during this "elimination period." This is the long-term-care version of a policy deductible. Again, you choose what this elimination period will be when you purchase your policy and pay premiums accordingly. Benefits can be paid for nursing and assisted living fees, home care services, necessary medical and home-safety equipment, and the like. Most policies have a total maximum payout amount, which varies with the quality of the policy. Lengthy or permanent stays at a nursing home or assisted living, or expensive home care fees, can cause a long-term-care policy to eventually max out, so know what you are buying initially. More than one hundred companies offered such policies in the 1990s, and they were prone to premium spikes to cover unanticipated benefits-cost overruns due to age creep in the US population. Now there are fewer than fifteen large carriers writing these policies.

Insurance companies have come up with a new model that combines whole life insurance with long-term care, so-called hybrid policies that will return money to your heirs if you wind up not needing long-term care. The premium is locked in up front and allows those who are older or have health problems a chance to qualify. The catch is that these policies are way more expensive. While the premium for a fifty-five-year-old couple buying a traditional long-term-care policy would be about $2,100 annually, a hybrid policy would cost $8,100. The costs for a sixty-five-year-old couple is even higher, $3,700 and $13,800, respectively, and the older you are when you purchase this type of insurance, the higher the costs. The good news is you can roll over an existing whole life policy or annuity to bring down the costs, and any benefits paid out generally are not taxed—the premiums are also deductible if you itemize your federal income taxes.

Most plans are purchased through insurance brokers, but some employers and professional organizations also offer them. The policies themselves usually require use of services from a licensed home care agency or licensed professional. Some will allow you to hire independent or nonlicensed providers or family members, but that varies by state. In addition to the types of care listed earlier, long-term-care policies also cover adult day care services and may provide coverage for services that are developed in the future.[15]

Though long-term-care policies cover a lot, they don't cover everything. You must read the fine print. Some policies include language that excludes coverage for things such as Alzheimer's disease, heart disease, diabetes, and some types of cancer. These policies are typically ineffective at covering home care or nursing services during a hospice event. A hospice patient typically passes before an assessment can qualify them and meet the time lapse of the elimination period.

But what happens if a family doesn't have long-term-care insurance and doesn't have the means to cover the costs? It's heartbreaking. The need is there whether the family can pay for it or not. It

---

15   Education & Outreach, "Understanding Long-Term Care Insurance," *AARP*, May 2016, https://www.aarp.org/health/health-insurance/info-06-2012/understanding-long-term-care-insurance.html.

doesn't go away. Some families turn to alternatives outside an agency, sometimes with disastrous result. They shop Craigslist and hire an anonymous caregiver privately, not realizing they're exposing themselves to workers' compensation risks if the caregiver gets injured, unemployment claims if the loved one passes and the caregiver doesn't have another job lined up, and prosecution if they don't comply with federal withholding rules. Additionally, they generally don't have the means to run background checks. People often do not realize that in most private-hire situations, that person you are paying becomes your employee, and you are the employer with all the responsibilities of such. It's not worth it. Many have realized that it is simply more cost, risk, and time efficient to hire a licensed agency.

Horror stories abound in this realm. Sometimes the caregiver will be in the home long enough to get the client to change a will or start stealing possessions or empty bank accounts. Then there are finders' fees, sometimes paid both by the caregiver and the client. If a month later the caregiver wants to take a vacation or just doesn't show up, you're out of luck. A licensed agency will provide a replacement at no additional cost or inconvenience to the client.

When we hire a caregiver, we run a thorough background check that complies with the Illinois Health Care Worker Background Check Act and a second check according to BrightStar Care standards. Our employees must provide their fingerprints, which are then run through the state database to determine whether they ever have been convicted of certain crimes, including unlawful restraint, battery, food tampering, theft, forgery, robbery, and arson.[16]

So what's a family to do? Plan for the inevitable.

---

16 "Disqualifying Convictions," Health Care Worker Registry, Illinois Department of Public Health, accessed July 10, 2019, http://www.idph.state.il.us/nar/disconvictions. htm.

WHAT TO DO

Early on, Judy and I went to a prospective client's home to do an assessment. We went through the procedure and came up with a care plan. The family looked at it and realized they didn't have the money to pay for it. They had made no provisions. The situation was heartbreaking since the deep need for care did not go away just because they could not pay for it! Judy and I discussed the matter on the sad trip back to the office that evening. The insurance people had been trying to sell us long-term-care coverage for a long time, and until that evening I had remained tone deaf about it. Judy and I went right out and purchased long-term policies for ourselves the same week.

My folks are a great example when it comes to planning ahead. When I was a small child, I can remember my dad on the phone with other local church leaders discussing "buying land for the retirement home." Their dream and planning eventually became a reality when Fairlawn Haven in Archbold, Ohio, came out of the ground. This retirement center continued to expand into assisted living, advanced rehab services, and a recreation/therapy building. Maybe most important for our family is that they ringed the complex with many duplex buildings that are considered independent-living units.

> The situation was heartbreaking since the deep need for care did not go away just because they could not pay for it!

Dad at times served on the board at the complex. I believe his experience with all this caused him to plan, or "track," in the direction of him and Mom living there in their later life. And that's exactly what happened. In fact, my parents made the move to those independent-living duplexes when Dad was in his early sixties. Due to his long-term perspective, our family did not have the hard discussions with parents when the time to transition is obvious to everyone but the seniors involved. Our family was spared all that.

The time to discuss these things is long before a loved one turns eighty-five and is stubbornly resisting any move. Retirement communities have graduated levels of care. The most basic are independent-living units or apartments. From there, a resident can move on to assisted living and when the need arises, skilled care. These communities provide a safe environment and a consistent care continuum. The apartments are built to incorporate senior safety standards. And if there's a medical event, many times it can be handled on-site. The resident sometimes transitions from independent living to nursing care and back to independent living.

Dad went directly from the duplexes to the highest level of care. Unfortunately, he was in long-term nursing care for four years until his passing several years ago.

More typically, unlike Dad's situation, there's a graduated ascension of care needs. The point is, we didn't have a family crisis at which we were required to sit down and figure out what to do. The plan was in place. Care flowed smoothly. Dad already had decided how he would spend his later years. As I write this book, Mom is now eighty-four and in a safe place. She's still living independently in the duplex where it all began. They have informal check-ins to monitor her well-being. There are times when I muse, "Mom could move in with us. We have the room and capacity. But that would involve interrupting what is a very competent later life care plan. It most likely would not be the correct thing to do."

The effects on the senior during transition of care, especially when a physical move is involved, vary immensely. Some seem relatively unaffected when a major life change such as moving occurs. Some are mildly inconvenienced and irritated for an intermittent time period. For others, it is a most jarring experience with commensurate risks.

We had one client who was living at a continuing-care retirement community (CCRC) in an independent-living duplex. We had provided her with live-in care for several years so she could remain in the lovely duplex and not have to move to assisted living. There came a day, however, when it was deemed necessary for her to make that very move. As the day came closer, the woman's health began failing. She was hospitalized several times, going from hospital to rehab to hospital and back. She passed without ever having seen the inside of the assisted living accommodations that had been prepared for her. Apparently, the threat of the move was too much for her to handle. I visited her several times when she was in the nursing home after discharge from the various hospitalizations. I can remember sitting in that room with her just wondering why it had to be that way, and there, of course, are no answers. Every senior is different to a degree on how he or she tolerates change such as that, especially those of advanced age and medical acuity.

Then there are the rare cases where someone moves from assisted living back home. We had one woman who loved her home, but she fell in the middle of winter and wound up lying on the floor overnight in the breezeway between her garage and her house. A family member found her the next day and called an ambulance. At least she hadn't broken anything. While she was hospitalized, the family called us. We were there when she came home. The family decided she should move into a beautiful local independent-living community. She moved, but a few days later we got a call from the grandkids. They said they needed our services again. Grandma had checked herself out of the independent-living facility and was back home. I can still remember what the granddaughter said in her call to us: "We got a call, and when we looked at the caller ID and it was Grandma's old number, we knew what she had done!" She took it upon herself and chose to be at home.

Baby boomers should be discussing these issues now, not waiting until they're incapacitated. We don't seem to realize or anticipate when we're healthy how matters of health will affect our life at the end.

A gentleman who lives near us is about the same age as Judy. He built his home a few years ago and had been planning to stay in it long term. But recently he developed some health problems. His hips were preventing him from walking. He decided to have a replacement, but during the preliminary examinations, doctors found a heart condition and wanted to put the surgery off for a year. He is a gardener and his hip problem was really interfering with what he loved doing. He was using a golf cart to get from the front of the house to the back. After six months, the all clear was given for his hip operation (although sometimes there comes a point when doctors refuse to do surgeries for bionic parts based on health matters).

> But a funny thing happens as people age: the longer they live, the longer they're expected to live.

Since then, his whole outlook has changed. He sold his sports car, a sweet little MG. He says he doesn't want to acquire any more things. They are selling the house with plans to move into something much more turnkey. He's gone from being very open to things to less so—all in less than a year based on a preliminary health event.

Things happen later in life, but people just don't want to think about it. You have to, though. Start with family discussions. Make sure family members know your desires. Get an estate planner involved and put acceptable plans in place.

LONGEVITY

Average life expectancy for women in North America was eighty-one in 2018 and for men, seventy-seven.[17] The Office of National Statistics estimates one in three babies born today will live to see one hundred. But a funny thing happens as people age: the longer they live, the longer they're expected to live.

According to the Office for National Statistics, here are some average life expectancies for women and men.[18] The column on the left shows a person's age, and the column on the right shows the age that person is expected to live to. For instance, women between ages sixty-five and seventy-three can expect to live to age eighty-nine. Men age sixty-five can expect to live to age eighty-six.

17   Erin Duffin, "Average Life Expectancy* in North America for Those Born in 2018, by Gender and Region (in Years)," accessed June 24, 2019, https://www.statista.com/statistics/274513/life-expectancy-in-north-america/.

18   "What Are Your Chances of Living to 100?" Office for National Statistics, January 14, 2016, https://www.ons.gov.uk/peoplepopulationand-community/birthsdeathsandmarriages/lifeexpectancies/articles/whatareyourchancesoflivingto100/2016-01-14.

WOMEN		MEN	
Age	**Age Expectation**	**Age**	**Age Expectation**
65–73	89	65	86
74	90	70	87
80	91	75	88
85	92	80	90
90	95	85	92
95	98	90	94
100	102	95	98
		100	102

Quality of life becomes a factor, and, for that reason, a plan should be in place well before extreme age sets in. The decision then becomes whether to age in place, enter a CCRC, move in with family, or choose another option.

In the past, what were called "old-age homes" were sometimes depressing places. Chronically understaffed, they would essentially warehouse the elderly. You can fill in the blanks here with your own stories of concern about nursing homes, founded or unfounded. It wasn't pretty. Elder abuse wasn't yet a very well-developed concept.

Fear of being housed in such facilities has led many parents to extract a promise from their children not to send them to a nursing home—ever. It became family policy and, in my opinion, at times to the detriment to their senior loved one.

I know of a family that would drive by Windsor Park Manor, a five-hundred-unit CCRC in Carol Stream that has been highly rated by U.S. News & World Report.[19] This community provides multiple levels of care as well as concierge services, activities like concerts and parties, a learning center, fitness center, and walking trails. This family would drive by and point to the complex, telling their mom, "That's a nursing home. You'll never have to see the inside," without realizing what was available.[20] Many CCRCs are beautiful, providing residents with rich, fulfilling, active lives. We took care of their mom in the home, but was she missing something by the family's mistaken understanding of the high level of care provided by many CCRCs?

Generally, the decision on whether someone should stay in his or her home or check into assisted living or a skilled-care facility depends on the level of care needed. Injections, wound care, physical therapy, help with glucose readings and insulin, and infusions are better handled at a skilled facility. A typical diabetic requires injections four times a day. A CNA cannot dose or administer this regimen. That would require a nurse at around sixty dollars a visit. In a skilled-nursing facility, the nurse is providing insulin and other skilled medical services to groups of people, eliminating the single visit expenses. Our agency, of course, can provide the nursing support—but it requires the family to pay privately for it.

Skilled-nursing-home services break down along two tracks: the short-term rehab track and long-term care. Insurance—Medicare plus supplemental coverage—generally covers rehab and for up to one hundred days. After that, it's considered long-term care and the patient or state-funded Medicaid is responsible.[21]

---

19   "Windsor Park Manor," *U.S. News & World Report*, accessed July 10, 2019, https://health.usnews.com/best-nursing-homes/area/il/windsor-park-manor-145606.

20   "Make the Most of Our Marvelous Windsor Park Lifestyle," Windsor Park, a Covenant Retirement Community, accessed July 10, 2019, https://www.windsor-parkillinois.org/independent-living-carol-stream-il.

21   "Your Medicare Coverage," Medicare.gov, accessed July 10, 2019, https://www.medicare.gov/coverage/skilled-nursing-facility-care.html.

Patient loads at a skilled-nursing facility can be problematic. Staffing levels very often are determined by the proportion of Medicaid patients. In Illinois, the state is notoriously slow in paying its bills, and then when it runs low on money, it starts discounting the payments for services that already have been performed. The service and financial pressures on facilities are enormous.

CCRCs are in a somewhat better position. Some are endowment communities, meaning that to get in, a resident has to pay a hefty entrance fee, which is in addition to the monthly fees for housing and services. That fee goes into a pool that helps cover the cost of skilled care. A resident can stay in the community no matter the level of care needed. It's a compelling value proposition, and for those that can afford it, it certainly allows for peace of mind.

The pricing can get complicated. One community in our area has multiple levels of buy-in: the bigger the up-front entrance fee, the lower the monthly housing cost, and vice versa. Another community, on the other hand, has a single pricing plan, making it easier for potential residents to understand. That's why planning ahead is so important: you don't want to be crunching the numbers at the last minute when care may be desperately needed. There is also the matter of availability of space when the time of need arises. Many times, we care for clients in their home while a waiting list clears to get them access to a senior community.

HIRING A CAREGIVER

Most home care agencies, after doing the initial client assessment, will determine which of their personnel would be the best fit. We believe you are hiring the agency along with its practices and standards. You have to trust us to provide a caregiver who will meet or exceed what's needed. BrightStar Care has a compatibility guarantee. We recognize certain personalities match up better than others, and we strive to provide the right fit. We have some clients who want their homes to be as quiet as a church. Others are very loud households. If it's too quiet, the client is not happy. We try pick up on those matters and match our personnel accordingly.

You definitely should ask questions about the agency and caregiver: not personal questions but questions concerning agency standards, insurance limits, prior work experience, competencies, and whether employees are W-2 employees or contractors.

Generally, family members have preconceived ideas about what they want in a caregiver. As it usually turns out, inevitably the first person we put in the home gets along well with everybody. We've had instances where we had to put in some people temporarily until a permanent caregiver could be assigned. Then we get a call wondering where the temporary caregivers went because the client and family liked them all!

We get a feel for what a client really wants during the assessment, and because we know our caregivers quite well, it's relatively simple to figure out who would be best in any given situation. That said, assigning a caregiver becomes a scheduling issue. The perfect caregiver for any given case might be tied up with other clients and/or not available for the assignment. It really is like a giant jigsaw puzzle—and the pieces keep moving and changing shapes.

If someone calls with a concern about a caregiver, we try to determine whether there's a need to change the caregiver or the care plan or whether there's an issue that's easy to correct. For example, maybe the client doesn't like someone hovering during bathroom visits and wants the door closed. If the family is OK with that, we'll tell the caregiver to back off. Other times it really is a personality clash.

We'll assign someone else. We tell our caregivers to remember what the family is going through. We're just alongside to help meet their needs, for however long that will be.

Family members, especially spouses, think they should be caregivers for their loved ones, but they don't realize the heavy toll that can take. We can provide respite care for a few hours a day to give that spouse / primary caregiver a break to take care of himself or herself.

> Family members, especially spouses, think they should be caregivers for their loved ones, but they don't realize the heavy toll that can take.

Unfortunately, what often happens is that the primary caregiver ignores his or her own needs, to everyone's detriment.

We had one woman who was taking care of her ailing husband. He had Parkinson's disease and was a fall risk. We were there to help from 8:00 a.m. to 2:00 p.m. and from 6:00 p.m. to 10:00 p.m. Then she was diagnosed with advanced cancer. She was unable to continue providing care for him. So we transitioned from hourly care to a live-in. And then she, previously the primary caregiver for her husband, passed away. He's still with us, but she is gone, and we see this aspect in our client families all too frequently.

When Judy and I still were operating out of our first office, which was in the basement of an office building, a gentleman walked in one day. He looked exhausted. He had been providing constant care for his wife, who had deep dementia and at times could turn violent. He needed a break. He hired us for three or four hours a day. He needed that time for himself.

Former First Lady Rosalynn Carter has said there are only four kinds of people in the world: those who have been caregivers, those who currently are caregivers, those who will be caregivers, and those who will need caregivers. By the time adults hit age sixty-five, most are dealing with at least one chronic condition; at seventy-five, two; and at eighty-five, three or more.

The Society of Certified Senior Advisors notes there are five levels of caregiving, often provided by a family member. In general, women are burdened with the highest levels of caregiving. Many have no help, and their efforts are complicated by their age and health problems.[22] And the care recipient may make matters worse. Often care recipients are upset by their conditions, concerned about financial resources, and fearful of losing their independence. Caregivers face emotional stress, physical strain, and financial hardship as a result of the time they're devoting. Sometimes this can result in abuse and neglect.

To relieve some of this stress, caregivers can turn to the following:
- Home health aides / home care services
- Housekeeping and chore services
- Care managers
- Financial advisers
- Insurance managers
- Neighbors
- Church volunteers
- Senior centers
- Transportation services
- Friendly visitors or companions
- Telephone reassurance programs
- Home maintenance and repair services

---

22 "Caregivers and Caregiving in America," The Society of Certified Senior Advisors, pp. 174–184, accessed July 10, 2019, https://www.csa.us/.

- Gatekeeper or home observation programs
- Personal emergency-response systems
- Hospice care
- Adult day care or night-care programs
- Meal-delivery services

Caregivers must recognize they have their own needs and be willing to delegate responsibilities to others to achieve some very much needed "me time."

LIVING WITH TERMINAL ILLNESS

Many people live with serious, chronic illnesses such as cancer, heart disease, ALS, kidney disease, AIDS, emphysema, diabetes, COPD, MS, and Parkinson's. But they want to keep on living. They are not ready to call it quits! They want help dealing with the stresses associated with their conditions to improve the quality of their lives. Many times, this means what they really need is palliative care.

Palliative care relieves symptoms associated with a disease. It's provided by an interdisciplinary team—doctor, nurse, pharmacist, social worker, dietitian, and volunteers—to treat the whole patient. The focus is on alleviating suffering. It doesn't mean a patient is giving up. In fact, sometimes palliative care given while a patient is undergoing treatment may help cure or reverse the effects of the illness. It helps patients cope with aggressive treatments.

Hospice care is a subset of palliative care and usually is provided if a patient is expected to live no longer than six months.[23]

Hospice is a philosophy of care, generally not a place. It addresses a patient's physical, emotional, social, and spiritual needs and helps a

---

23   "Frequently Asked Questions about Hospice and Palliative Care," Palliative Doctors, accessed July 10, 2019, http://palliativedoctors.org/faq.

patient's family caregivers, focusing as much on the family as the patient, providing grief services. Following a death, counseling is available for thirteen months. Hospice care can be delivered in a patient's home rather than a facility, although there are actual brick-and-mortar sites. It concentrates on managing pain and other symptoms to allow patients to live as fully as possible until the end.

> Hospice is a philosophy of care, generally not a place.

By now you can see that the world of health care is very complex, and yet amid all the complexities, it's crucial to uphold the standards of quality care. After all, we're dealing with people's lives. That's one reason why we chose to be medically licensed and work maintain Joint Commission accreditation.

CHAPTER 7

Why Medical Expertise Is Important

There's a big difference between nonmedical and medically licensed home care agencies. We are defined by our medical licensure even though most of our clients technically require nonmedical service. The number of nonmedically licensed agencies dwarfs those, such as us, that are medically licensed. But our medical licensing coupled with Joint Commission accreditation is the gold standard.

Much of the care of our nonmedical clients could be handled by family, but some clients have no family, and there are other cases where family just doesn't have the bandwidth to take care of another's needs. In cases where family does provide the bulk of the care, those caregivers sometimes just need a break. It's a chaotic business that's ever changing, be it because a client gets better and no longer needs our services or worsens and requires hospitalization or long-term care in a skilled-nursing facility. Meeting patients' caregiving needs never reaches stasis; it's ever changing.

When a client contracts us for skilled nursing, however, the situation is quite different. Family members, unless one or more of them has nursing skills, are ill equipped to meet patient needs.

Clients may need a live-in caregiver or twenty-four-hour service when discharged from the hospital. They'll need help with daily living, including meal prep—something nonmedical agencies can handle. But they probably will also go home with wounds or a medication regimen that will need daily tending, and many times Medicare won't cover that, putting the burden on the family. Agencies that don't have medical competencies won't be able to help them because licensure does not allow nonmedical caregivers to handle such things. We, on the other hand, have the capacity to send a nurse in to do dressing changes or whatever other skilled-nursing care is necessary. Our nurses are most likely better equipped than family members to follow doctors' orders on such matters.

Early on, I joined the Association of Senior Service Providers for DuPage County. I'd go to the meetings, and the attendees would introduce themselves at the start of the meetings. Most of the attendees would describe their businesses as "nonmedical home care agencies." Even though I didn't know much back then, I would stand up and say, "Jim Flickinger, BrightStar Care of Central DuPage–Wheaton. We are a skilled medical home care agency." Even the sound of that showed our business had significantly more professional gravitas and skilled clinical weight. Skilled medical licensure is much harder to get and requires a demonstration of organizational medical competency and medically trained / licensed personnel. You have to demonstrate those things before the agency will be licensed. I think being medically licensed is our greatest strength. It is also the overall BrightStar Care standard (i.e., in the states where medical licensure is an option, the local BrightStar Care agency will obtain such). BrightStar Care is simply a much better service model because of our system-wide medical competencies. The Joint Commission agrees and has awarded its rare Enterprise Champion of Quality award to BrightStar Care system-wide for many years now.

Margherita C. Labson, executive director of the Joint Commission's Home Care Accreditation program, said in a blog post that BrightStar Care is "at the cutting edge of home-based care services." The award recognizes BrightStar Care for demonstrating a proven commitment to delivering the highest quality of care and safety, adhering to the principles of continuous quality improvement, and having 95 percent of its franchisees fully accredited and in good standing.

THE JOINT COMMISSION

We received our Joint Commission seal in 2011, and it was an important achievement, not only organizationally but also with our referral sources. The Joint Commission is a high-practice accrediting organization that started out primarily concentrating on specialized medicine and hospitals. After a while, it made sense for the organization to start looking at home health and home care agencies since more medical care is tracking to the home and outside the traditional hospitals and skilled-nursing facilities. The accreditation assures our referral sources, especially those in medical establishments, that we have the same goals they do in terms of quality of care.

The Joint Commission's mission is to improve patient safety. To that end, it developed a set of national patient safety goals using input from its Patient Safety Advisory Group, which is composed of doctors, pharmacists, risk managers, clinicians, and other professionals working in a wide variety of care settings.

There are five goals for home care:

1. Identify patients correctly: use at least two ways to identify patients. For example, use the patient's name and date of birth. This is done to make sure that each patient gets the correct medicine and treatment.

2. Use medicines safely: record and pass along all correct information about a patient's medicines. Find out what medicines the patient is taking. Compare those medicines to new medicines given to the patient. Make sure the patient knows which medicines to take when they are at home. Tell the patient it is important to bring their up-to-date list of medicines every time they visit a doctor.

3. Prevent infection: use the hand cleaning guidelines from the Centers for Disease Control and Prevention or the World Health Organization. Set goals for improving hand cleaning. Use the goals to improve hand cleaning.

4. Prevent patients from falling: find out which patients are most likely to fall. For example, is the patient taking any medicines that might make them weak, dizzy, or sleepy? Take action to prevent falls for these patients.

5. Identify patient safety risks: find out if there are any risks for patients who are getting oxygen. For example, fires in the patient's home.[24]

Initially, I wasn't thrilled with the idea of inviting yet another oversight body into the operations of our business. Plus, I knew before we even started the initial accreditation process that it would involve a large time commitment and monetary expense. Then we started going through the initial training and mock surveys, and along the way, I caught the vision of it all. It was an incredible undertaking for our organization.

Our initial Joint Commission assessment was a two-day event

---

24 "2018 Home Care National Patient Safety Goals," the Joint Commission, accessed July 10, 2019, https://www.jointcommission.org/assets/1/6/2018_OME_NPSG_ goals_final.pdf.

that was performed by a person who had recently surveyed two other BrightStar Care agencies in another state. She had developed a pattern of looking for certain aspects she found problematic in our model, and of course she found them at our organization as well. She cited us for eleven things she deemed deficient in our operation. Even though we were new to this accreditation process, something did not sit right with me on several of those findings. I went through the formal process of challenging eight of the findings. The Joint Commission agreed with four of the challenges, which left us with seven matters to improve upon after the initial survey.

Of the remaining findings, there were a few that I absolutely agreed with. We had not been as thorough as we should have been with medical-record dating and signatures. In another example, Joint Commission standards required fifteen points of patient or patient families' education upon initial start of patient care. That included issues such as explaining the plan of care, oral health, and basic physical and structural safety. We were doing that, but we hadn't documented it very well. In another instance, we had not properly closed out a patient record by issuing a discharge summary. The surveyor also wanted us to develop a comprehensive statement of what comprises a patient record, such as an emergency-contact form, the patient assessment, the plan of care, and the discharge summary. As we corrected these matters and showed the Joint Commission such, we improved our organizational and patient-care processes, which are exactly the intended outcomes of the accreditation process. It provides yet another level of assurance for our clients.

We have now done three Joint Commission surveys, and the number of findings is not much of an issue. Rather, these surveys have become on-site process-improvement collaborations. We don't just look at the metrics of these inspections. We use these metrics to improve our outcomes and care processing. What's helped a lot in improving documentation is that we've moved from paper to a computerized program. It's a much more efficient and thorough method of handling things.

As I mentioned, our accreditation is important to our referral sources, but regulations prevent those sources from just telling patients to call us. Gone are the days when we brought doughnuts and cupcakes to doctors' offices to ingratiate ourselves. Now it's all about patient choice. Many times, the patient's family member is handed a list of agencies that provide care, and it's up to the patient or the patient's family to investigate the choices. We have some concerns with this approach to choosing something as important as critical health care. It is our role to raise awareness of our unique capabilities with the public and health care providers in our market space. Then, recognizing our name on a list in a time of need means something.

BrightStar Healthcare of Dupage-Wheaton

Wheaton, IL

has been Accredited by

The Joint Commission

Which has surveyed this organization and found it to meet the requirements for the

Home Care Accreditation Program

August 23, 2017

Accreditation is customarily valid for up to 36 months.

ID #507888
Print/Reprint Date: 10/18/2017

Craig W. Jones, FACHE
Chair, Board of Commissioners

Mark R. Chassin, MD, FACP, MPP, MPH
President

The Joint Commission is an independent, not-for-profit national body that oversees the safety and quality of health care and other services provided in accredited organizations. Information about accredited organizations may be provided directly to The Joint Commission at 1-800-994-6610. Information regarding accreditation and the accreditation performance of individual organizations can be obtained through The Joint Commission's web site at www.jointcommission.org.

It's always been important to somehow inform the people who have direct contact with our potential patients. That could be a hospital nurse, social worker, posthospitalization planner, or someone at a skilled-nursing or rehab facility. These folks must have confidence in us to care for their precious patient before they will suggest that we can help. Clients have told me they were overwhelmed by the whole hospitalization/rehab and discharge process and asked a nurse on the floor to tell them what to do. In those cases, a nurse knowing our capabilities would guide a patient toward us. We always ask new clients how they heard of us, and then we find means to thank the person making the referral.

STATE LICENSURE

Of course, the most important pieces of paper an agency frames and hangs on the wall are the licenses issued by the state where you do business. In our case, that is the state of Illinois. Our experiences with this prime licensing body for us have been equally positive. The Illinois Department of Public Health (IDPH) has the organizational slogan of "Protecting health, improving lives," and generally I believe they are doing just that. We initially obtained, and now maintain, two separate licenses from IDPH: a home-services license, which encompasses most of the caregiving functions we do in the home, and the more complex home-nursing license, which allows us to perform skilled medical services. It is my belief this second license tier for application of skilled services is a game changer. It causes us to execute our entire agency through the higher competency of a medical establishment. We are fortunate that from day one we operated under both of these license levels.

> It is my belief this second license tier for application of skilled services is a game changer.

Illinois has a somewhat strict list of patient services that can be performed by nonmedical and medically licensed personnel. Nonmedical personnel typically perform things like meal preparation, light housekeeping, companion activities, bathing, and a certain modest level of personal care, well-being checks, and the like.

Then comes skilled services, which are done under our nursing license. While the list of services we provide under this license is robust and complex, the basics are wound care, medication management, catheter care, blood draws and injections, hospice nursing services, and infusion therapy. Performing these services starts with a licensed nurse, with specific competencies matched to the skilled service provided.

HEALTH CARE CAREERS

If someone is interested in a medical career, a good first step is CNA training. That's building block number one. The next level is to become a licensed practical nurse (LPN). Everything studied as a CNA gets recognized and pulled forward into an LPN program. That step requires more coursework, clinical work, and training. The next step is a registered nurse (RN). Generally everything studied up to that point is applicable. RNs receive another level of training and clinical work so they can perform their medical functions unsupervised. As health services have become more complex, most hospitals now require their RNs to have bachelor's degrees in nursing (BSNs), which require more coursework to ensure a more well-rounded education and more of a chance to advance into management. There are also master's and doctoral programs for nurses, who can go on to become nurse practitioners and physicians' assistants.

Our CNAs are directly supervised by our nursing staff.

CNAs provide basic patient care and can assist in daily activities like bathing and dressing. Other duties include the following:

- Reporting changes in a patient's condition and needs, including inputs and outputs, weight, and appetite
- Taking vital signs like temperature, blood pressure, pulse, respirations

- Housekeeping services related to medical needs
- Skin care using nonmedicated or nonprescription products
- Assisting with ambulation, whether the patient is walking on his or her own or using adaptive equipment like a walker, cane, or wheelchair
- Bathing assistance, including for patients whose skin is not intact
- Assisting with dressing, including doctor-prescribed support stockings if the CNA has been trained and competency tested
- Assisting with exercise and encouraging patient to perform a prescribed exercise program
- Performing simple procedures as an extension of therapeutic services
- Assisting with normal feeding of patients
- Assisting with personal grooming and mouth care
- Assisting with positioning
- Helping client bathroom functions
- Changing clothing and pads used for incontinence matters
- Assisting with all types of transfers as long as the CNA has been trained and competency tested for the equipment used
- Reminding client to take medications and directly observing whether the medication was taken

Anything more complicated or requiring medication administration or an injection, such as insulin shots and other injections, needs to be done by a nurse.

Ninety percent of our in-home business is what would be termed nonmedical home services. That being said, our medical licensure allows us to perform those functions at a much higher level. Even in a nonmedical service situation, we are in a position to be aware of medical conditions that might need to be reported to a family member or our supervisory nurse. Our skilled plan assessments are very sophisticated documents signed by an RN that also must be approved by a patient's primary care doctor.

It really shows you what medical home care involves. It's a collaboration that enables our patients to maintain conditions at home and enjoy a better level of health. Even our nonmedical cases get plans of care developed by an RN. We train our nonmedical caregivers to pick up certain signs of medical conditions. It gives us a leg up to act if a patient's condition changes.

MAINTAINING A HIGH-QUALITY STAFF

We work hard to hire and retain our caregivers, CNAs, and nurses—and many CNAs want to be nurses. I give them a lot of credit for wanting to extend their educations, but at the same time, it creates staff-retention matters for us. We have learned that generally the health care employment field is, shall we say, more "fluid" than many other professions. It just seems the health care group is quite comfortable moving around a lot! With the business volume our organization has had from the beginning, that creates internal staffing shortages on a regular basis, hence the need for perpetual large-volume recruiting activities.

Once somebody is hired, the goal is to retain our staff. To that end, we give out Employee of the Month and Employee of the Year awards. We also host an open house and a referral luncheon where we encourage staff to bring a friend interested in working for us. If the friend is hired, the employee gets a referral bonus. We have other incentives as well. Our employees earn vacation time accrued through hours worked. We offer a funded 401(k) plan. We have continually received the Employer of Choice award from Home Care Pulse, our industry's leader in quality surveying.[25]

---

25 "2018 Best of Home Care Award-Winners," *Best of Home Care*, accessed July 10, 2019, https://www.bestofhomecare.com/award-winners/2018/.

Our staff tell us the continuing education program is a big plus, especially now that it's on the internet and easily accessible. But education really occurs on a daily basis. Our nursing staff is always available to help caregivers when they run into challenging situations. For example, we had a dementia patient who began exhibiting more aggressive behavior toward our caregiver. One of our nurse case managers talked to the caregiver about methods of handling the behavior and printed out articles on the subject to help the caregiver handle the situation. We make sure staff can handle whatever situations come their way, whether that means talking with the family, providing more training, or changing the care plan. Our field staff gets a lot of education on handling chronic illnesses, mostly in what to look for and who should be notified of changes.

One of the biggest obstacles to retaining employees is health insurance. It's expensive because an individual franchise is a relatively small operation when it comes to group policies. A caregiver making ten to fourteen dollars an hour has a tough time affording premiums that run into the multiple hundreds of dollars.

PATIENT SAFETY

Patients, especially those in the pre–baby boom generation, often are reluctant to question their health care matters, especially from their doctors. We believe there are times where patients, maybe with their families, need to assess their care and make course corrections, if needed. The Joint Commission agrees with this approach. It developed a Speak Up initiative in 2002 in conjunction with the Centers for Medicare & Medicaid Services and relaunched it in May 2018. The campaign's goal is to help patients and their advocates be more active in their care.[26] It includes not only print materials and posters but videos that can be used as public service announcements that are available on the Joint Commission's YouTube channel[27] and website.[28]

Speak Up Is an Acronym

S	**Speak up** if you have questions or concerns. If you still don't understand, ask again. It's your body and you have a right to know.
P	**Pay attention** to the care you get. Always make sure you're getting the right treatments and medicines by the right health care professionals. Don't assume anything.
E	**Educate yourself** about your illness. Learn about the medical tests you get—and your treatment plan.
A	**Ask** a trusted family member or friend to be your advocate (adviser or supporter).
K	**Know** what medicines you take and why you take them. Medicine errors are the most common health care mistakes.[29]

Credit: "Facts about Speak Up initiatives," the Joint Commission, 2012.

26 "Speak Up about Your Care," the Joint Commission, accessed July 10, 2019, https://www.jointcommission.org/speakup.aspx.

27 "The Joint Commission," YouTube, accessed July 10, 2019, https://www.youtube.com/user/TheJointCommission.

28 "Videos," the Joint Commission, accessed July 10, 2019, https://www.jointcommission.org/multimedia/.

29 "Facts about Speak Up initiatives," the Joint Commission, October 2012, https://www.jointcommission.org/assets/1/6/Facts_Speak_Up.pdf.

In addition, the Joint Commission advises using a hospital, clinic, surgery center, or other type of health care organization that has been carefully checked out, like those that have been assessed by the commission for quality. It also advises participating in all decisions about treatment.

A survey of nearly 1,900 organizations indicated 85 percent said the campaign and others like it improve the accreditation and certification process, and 80 percent gave the program high marks as a means of improving communication with both patients and staff about safety issues.[30]

The original brochures covered such issues as infection prevention, patient rights, and how to avoid medication errors. Some organizations put the Speak Up materials in patient rooms.

The program helps patients understand they are partially responsible for the quality of their health care. If they have concerns or questions, they should voice them—especially when it comes to medication interactions. Too often patients have not spoken up, and that's been detrimental to their care. This is the crux of our interest and involvement with our patients in scrutinizing the best care for them.

---

30 "Facts about Speak Up initiatives," the Joint Commission, October 2012, https://
www.jointcommission.org/assets/1/18/Speak_Up_Oct_2012.pdf.

CHAPTER 8

Staffing Services

Though in-home care is our core business, we have staffing contracts with many facilities, everything from schools to retirement communities, health care facilities to hospice organizations, memory care facilities to churches. Many use us heavily on a daily, shift-by-shift basis. Others call us for staffing sporadically. Some have yet to call us for actual services but want to have a staffing services plan in place.

Generally, such staffing is on an ad hoc basis with per diem shifts. It can be episodic and chaotic. But where we see truly successful staffing is when a client can tell us in advance what they need and for how long. That makes it much easier to manage the schedule. Our caregivers obtain a consistent schedule with guaranteed hours. They become familiar with the patients and are more committed to the job.

Our initial foray into providing staffing services came just a few months after we opened at a local residential home and school for the pediatric disabled. These people do God's work, caring for deeply disabled children.

I had paid a call on them early on, just a friendly visit. Our association with them began with occasional shifts, when a nurse would call in sick; then one went on maternity leave, and we filled the gap. It was vital that every time they called, we simply had to find staff and fill their request. They couldn't go without coverage, so the pressure was on for us. They put a lot of faith and trust in us at a time when we had yet to prove ourselves. But they could tell we were genuine, which I believe was a primary reason a lot of our early clients, both in private duty and staffing services, took a chance on us.

> They could tell we were genuine, which I believe was a primary reason a lot of our early clients, both in private duty and staffing services, took a chance on us.

Fast-forward six years, and in 2015 this center decided to outsource all of its twenty-four-hour nursing and much of its CNA work so that it could concentrate on core competencies. After several rounds of harrowing public bidding on the matter, we were fortunate to be awarded a five-year contract to provide for all the skilled-nursing services at the center.

This scenario is a single-facility example of how we grew and developed as a major medical-staffing organization providing medical personnel to tens of health care facilities in our business area. It started quite modestly but ballooned over time as our reputation for service and "filling the shifts" became well known. We have staffing-service contracts with almost every school district in our area. We provide service from multiple nurses daily to a single district when school is in session down to erstwhile service for some of the schools when they are shorthanded.

But by far our primary volume of staffing opportunities is with nursing / skilled facilities and assisted living centers that simply cannot hire enough personnel to meet their needs. Health care wonks for years have predicted a dire worker shortage based on many factors but primarily related to the aging of the baby boomer generation. That shortage started en masse around 2012, at least for our marketplace, and has been getting more acute over time.

The way it works is that a local facility calls us to fill a certain number of CNA and/or nurse shifts for them because they do not have staff to cover, and since we presumably are less short staffed than they are, we have reserve capacity to fill their requests. What this really means is that in an acute worker-shortage environment, we have slightly to significantly better recruiting and retention criteria in place to meet the staffing requests from our clients.

We have structured our business to separate this sometimes chaotic and very different service line from our home care division. That means separate recruiting lines, scheduling, and related business/services aspects. Staffing service just turns out to be so "otherly" that we keep it separate from the home care / medical lines of work.

In some ways, the staffing end of our business is not all that different from in-home care. For our employees, however, it can be more challenging because they are taking care of multiple patients. Since we began our operations, the shortage of health care workers continues to become more acute, presenting us with both opportunities and challenges. And as the situation worsens, just like the facilities we service, we still have to find employees willing to fill those needs. An edge we have is that we generally can provide a wider variety of assignments than one would get working in a single facility. Also, our people understand that when they come to work for us, they're working for a high-practice organization.

VENUE OF CARE—AT HOME OR IN A CARE COMMUNITY?

Our core is in providing services in the home. The decision on whether to remain in one's home or enter an independent-living or assisted living facility is a difficult one in which many factors are in play. The "nursing home" stigma has struck fear in people's hearts. But public attitudes are changing with the development of new communities that offer opportunities for the social interaction lacking when loved ones remain isolated in their homes. Some of the newer facilities are quite opulent.

> Our care plans are designed to keep a patient healthy and safe, thus reducing the need for hospitalizations and skilled facilities.

As nice as these places may be, they are not the same as the comfort and familiarization of home or the sense of freedom one experiences outside an institution. In a home situation, the caregiver gives his or her full attention to a single patient. The patient doesn't have to compete for help at any given moment. There's also less potential for the spread of disease and more ease in dealing with personal care and bathing issues. Our care plans are designed to keep a patient healthy and safe, thus reducing the need for hospitalizations and skilled facilities.

According to 2016 data from the Kaiser Family Foundation, more than 1.3 million people live in certified nursing facilities.[31]

---

31   "Total Number of Residents in Certified Nursing Facilities," Kaiser Family Foundation, accessed April 7, 2019, https://www.kff.org/other/state-indicator/number-of-nursing-facility-residents/?currentTimeframe=0&sortModel=%7B%22colId%22:%22Location%22,%22sort%22:%22asc%22%7D.

And the National Center for Assisted Living reports that more than 800,000 people are in assisted living, with an average length of stay of twenty-two months.[32] In independent living, the average was thirty-eight months; continuing-care retirement communities, seventy-seven months; and Alzheimer's care, seventeen months.[33] Of those living in assisted living communities, 34 percent will move to skilled-nursing care because of failing health, while 30 percent will pass away.[34] Within the first year of moving into a skilled-nursing facility, the death rate is as high as 60 percent, with the greatest percentage concentrated in the first six months, so transferring away from home, even if for failing health reasons, is a very serious matter.[35] We have seen the decline in many, many of our patients who left home for a facility.

In fact, numerous studies of the long-term-care industry find that people of any age in "institutional care" have shorter life spans than people who remain in their homes.[36] And it's more than just their health that leads to their demise; it's also the change in their living arrangements. More than additional exposure to disease, their "will to live" comes into play.[37]

---

32 "Residents," National Center for Assisted Living, accessed April 7, 2019, https://www.ahcancal.org/ncal/facts/Pages/Residents.aspx.

33 Chris Orestis, "Life Expectancy Compression: The Impact of Moving into a Long-Term Care Facility on Length of Life," Life Care Funding, February 12, 2013, http://www.lifecarefunding.com/white-papers/moving-into-long-term-care-facility/.

34 Ibid.

35 Ibid.

36 Ibid.

37 Ibid.

CARING FOR THE ELDERLY

Studies indicate patients who understand the value of their relationship with their health care provider feel more in control of their health and are not only more satisfied, but the care they receive improves their health overall.[38]

The goal is improved patient outcomes. When we can meet the client in the hospital or rehabilitation center before discharge, we work with the discharge nurse to make sure all needs will be met.

As the funding pressures increase on Medicare,[39] many people are being pushed into their homes where in the past they would have been funneled into a skilled-care facility. Some of the need for in-home care will be solved through telemetry and robotics. Patients who need kidney dialysis now have access to in-home systems. There's even a robotic caregiver that can lift a three-hundred-pound patient, but my advice is "Don't try that one at home alone!" Diagnostics like vital signs can be handled through telemetry.

In other cultures, the norm is for the elderly to move into their children's homes. That was generally the way it was in this country as recently as a generation ago. But in the United States, we have become very independent, and that attitude has affected our parents as well. Even in China, where the norm was to care for one's aging parents, the country's one-child policy has produced a more westernized society where those single children don't have anyone with whom to share the responsibility, nor do they have the time or the means to fulfill that

---

38 Vidya Sudhakar-Krishnan and Mary C. J. Rudolf, "How Important Is Continuity of Care?" *Archives of Disease in Children*, vol. 92, no. 5 (May 2007):381–383, accessed April 7, 2019, on US National Library of Medicine, National Institutes of Public Health, https://www.ncbi.nlm.nih.gov/pmc/articles/PMC2083711/.

39 Paul N. Van De Water, "Medicare Is Not 'Bankrupt,'" Center on Budget and Policy Priorities, July 3, 2018, https://www.cbpp.org/research/health/medicare-is-not-bankrupt.

obligation. The result has been a mass migration of Filipino caregivers to China, drying up the pool that used to flow to the United States and exacerbating the US shortage. China has even set up its own schools to train CNAs in the Philippines. Where would we all be without the loving caregiving of the Filipino people?

Closer to home, we used to recruit our CNAs and caregivers from a ten-mile radius of our office under the premise that their commute to our clients' homes would be shorter. But the truth is that we seem to have exhausted our recruiting resources locally. So we have widened the geographic area we recruit from, particularly for our staffing services division. We're not quite reaching into Indiana or Wisconsin yet in our recruiting, but we are reaching out in a twenty-five-mile radius and likely will have to expand that farther as the employment needs continue to grow.

Our efforts include postings on various job boards, working with health care schools in the area, and working with outside agencies, as well as rewarding current employees to bring a friend to us who is subsequently hired. But it is just flat out getting hard to find health-care-trained personnel, especially in a booming economy. Government projections indicate the situation is going to get worse for many years to come.

CHAPTER 9

The Future of Home Health Care

When I was looking for a new career at the height of the 2008 recession, I was looking for a business that would be sustainable no matter the overall economy. Something in the health care realm seemed to make the most sense, and as I researched the issue, I concluded geriatric care was going to be a growth area.

The US population is aging. By the middle of this century, 20 percent of the population is expected to be sixty-five and older.[40] The UN estimates the total US population at that point will number 404 million, while the US Census Bureau pegs it as high as 458 million, up 100 million from 2010, largely through immigration. Currently, the over-sixty-five crowd makes up just 13 percent of the population.

In 2011, the first of the 76 million Americans born during the baby boom, 1946–64, began reaching age sixty-five. The percentage of those eighty-five and older is expected to triple by 2050, growing from 1.4 percent of the population to 4.3 percent.[41] By 2035, those

---

40   Joel Kotkin, "The Changing Demographics of America," *Smithsonian Magazine*, August 2010, https://www.smithsonianmag.com/travel/the-changing-demographics-of-america-538284/.

41   "U.S. Demographic Shifts," Strategic Foresight Initiative, May 2011, https://www.fema.gov/pdf/about/programs/oppa/demography_%20paper_051011.pdf.

older than sixty-five are expected to outnumber the under-eighteen crowd 78 million to 76.4 million, a milestone in demographic shifts.[42]

Between 1900 and 2010, the proportion of the population sixty-five and older increased at an average rate of 0.74 percent per decade. In the next two decades, the rate will top 3 percent per year.[43]

The baby boom was not repeated when boomers entered their reproductive years, and birth rates also declined. Couple that with longer life expectancy, and it's not difficult to understand why the population is aging so rapidly.

The United States is not alone. Japan already has the world's oldest population, with those sixty-five and older making up a full quarter of the population (the United States is expected to reach that proportion by 2060). By midcentury, the number of Japanese is expected to shrink by twenty million. Europe is headed in the same direction.

Because of this age shift, the demand for in-home caregiving and assisted living facilities is expected to grow, especially for those suffering from Alzheimer's disease and other forms of memory issues in addition to those with physical infirmities.

A study looking at the needs and wants of the elderly in the Memphis, Tennessee, area in 2012 revealed people generally wanted to stay in their homes, but their residences needed to be retrofitted to make aging in place possible. However, making such improvements is costly, and many people cannot afford to make the necessary modifications.

---

42   Jonathan Vespa, "The U.S. Joins Other Countries with Large Aging Populations," US Census Bureau, March 13, 2018, revised September 6, 2018, https://www.census.gov/library/stories/2018/03/graying-america.html.

43   Robert M. Sade, "The Graying of America: Challenges and Controversies," *The Journal of Law, Medicine & Ethics*, vol. 40, no. 1 (Spring 2012): 6–9, accessed April 7, 2019, on US National Library of Medicine, National Institutes of Public Health, https://www.ncbi.nlm.nih.gov/pmc/articles/PMC4501019/.

The MetLife Foundation has since launched pilot studies to determine what changes are needed on the local level to improve the lives of seniors who want to remain in their homes.[44]

LIFE EXPECTANCY

Improvements in health care have increased the US life expectancy dramatically since the dawn of the twentieth century. People born in 1900 were not expected to live much past age 50. Now the average life expectancy is 78.8 years—81.2 for women and 76.4 for men—with 10 percent of females and 5 percent of males expected to live past age 100.[45]

Today's elderly population also is better off financially than their predecessors. In 1970, about 25 percent of seniors lived below the poverty line. By 2005, that had dropped to 10 percent—fully 2.6 percentage points less than the national average. In 2008, the median income for someone sixty-five or older was $18,208. Today, that has risen to $25,757—and that's with a sharp decline in the number of people collecting traditional pensions.

> Improvements in health care have increased the US life expectancy dramatically since the dawn of the twentieth century.

Though that increase in income is significant, it's inadequate to cover the costs of long-term care should it become necessary.

---

44 Kathy Moore Cowan, "The Graying of America: Preparing for What Comes Next," Federal Reserve Bank of St. Louis, fall 2013, https://www.stlouisfed.org/publications/bridges/fall-2013/the-graying-of-america-preparing-for-what-comes-next.

45 "Americans Are Living Longer," USC Leonard Davis School of Gerontology, https://gerontology.usc.edu/resources/infographics/americans-are-living-longer/.

Long-term care is for people with chronic illnesses, disabilities, or other conditions that make it necessary for them to need help on a daily basis for an extended period of time. The care can range from such simple activities as bathing to skilled care from medical professionals. That care comes with a price, whether an individual remains at home or enters assisted living or a skilled-nursing facility.

AGING IN PLACE

Deciding whether to live out the golden years in one's longtime residence or move into a senior residence facility can be a difficult choice that depends on many factors. Staying in one's home has many attractions, chief among them the memories created during one's lifetime.

But consideration also needs to be given to the appropriateness: Is there a support system on which one can rely? Does one have infirmities that will make getting around more difficult as one ages? Has the home been adequately upgraded for necessary safety? Can one afford to have caregivers come in to help? Can one handle the upkeep?

The decision is not easy. It's only natural to deny our bodies ever will grow weaker if we follow all the rules like eating right and exercising. We also don't want to think our mental acuity is slipping or that everyday tasks will grow increasingly more difficult. Taking care of a home grows more difficult too when it comes to cleaning out gutters or even changing a light bulb. And neighborhoods change, possibly making security an issue.

There's also the isolation factor. Once one is out of the workforce, does he or she have a means of meeting new people and making friends? As we age, our reflexes slow, which makes driving an issue. Cooking can become a chore, leading to poor nutrition.

Moving into various forms of retirement communities can mitigate the problems that develop as part of the aging process, providing everything from meals in dining rooms with other residents, transportation for shopping and other excursions, organized activities to relieve loneliness, round-the-clock security, and help with tasks like bathing and cleaning to care for chronic diseases and conditions.[46] But at the same time, there's a loss, perceived and real, of autonomy and independence. And if a person doesn't like the food, he or she is out of luck.

The decision must be made thoughtfully and carefully—and not just based on one's economic resources.

To remain successfully in one's home, especially an older home, steps need to be taken to make it more convenient and accessible, ranging from installing grab bars for toilets and tubs or showers, to changing door handles to the lever variety, to lowering light switches and raising outlets, to clearing away clutter and eliminating throw rugs, to widening doorways to accommodate walkers and wheelchairs. It also may even be necessary to install ramps and elevators.[47]

Once home modifications cease to be an issue, the next big question is maintenance. Is one physically able to take care of his or her property, or does he or she need to hire out when something needs doing, even the simple chores like vacuuming or unclogging a toilet? Consider whether there's anyone who can be called in an emergency.

There's no question that moving out of one's home into a senior residence of some sort will take adjustment, whether that's into an independent-living community or a skilled-nursing facility. Usually the space is smaller, so that means culling one's possessions and

---

46 "Nine Reasons Aging in Place May Not Be Right for You," *Senior Living*, https://www.seniorliving.com/article/nine-reasons-aging-place-may-not-be-right-you.

47 "Aging in Place versus Assisted Living," *Senior Living*, accessed July 10, 2019, https://www.seniorliving.com/article/aging-place-versus-assisted-living.

disposing of furniture. Then there's the fear of whether one will be able to make friends in a new environment.

A study by the Arizona State University College of Nursing indicated allowing seniors to age in place could be more cost effective for Medicare and Medicaid than requiring people to enter inpatient facilities, lowering costs by about $1,600 a month. The study examined the costs by comparing thirty-nine Midwest nursing facilities with thirty-nine people who remained in their homes.[48]

ELDERCARE

Nurses and nurse scientists have been in the forefront of eldercare and are expected to play an increasingly important role in developing strategies for allowing seniors to live as independently as possible for as long as possible. Nurses play a major role in frontline care, ranging from preventive care in primary care offices to acute care in hospitals to long-term care in skilled-nursing facilities and other senior living communities, as well as care during home visits.[49]

> Nurses play a major role in frontline care.

It is estimated that 80 percent of those sixty-five and older have at least one chronic illness such as heart disease, diabetes, or arthritis and that a substantial portion of the population has more than one, making disease management complex.

---

48 K. D. Marek et al., "Aging in Place versus Nursing Home Care: Comparison of Costs to Medicare and Medicaid," *Research in Gerontological Nursing*, vol. 5, no. 2 (April 2012): 123–29, accessed April 7, 2019, on US National Library of Medicine, National Institutes of Public Health, https://www.ncbi.nlm.nih.gov/pubmed/21846081.

49 Patricia A. Grady, "Advancing the Health of Our Aging Population: A Lead Role for Nursing Science," *Nursing Outlook*, vol. 59 (2011): 207–9, https://www.ninr.nih.gov/sites/files/docs/drgradynogeriatricnursingjuly20112.pdf.

These conditions often involve pain and impact quality of life as well as engender considerable economic costs and place burdens not only on the patient but on family and friends who provide for his or her care. Throw in dementia, and the problems grow geometrically.

An estimated sixteen million caregivers provide unpaid care for loved ones with Alzheimer's disease. In 2018, they provided an estimated 18.5 billion hours of care.[50] This is a staggering figure! And those statistics are expected to grow astronomically as baby boomers continue to age. As conditions worsen, untrained family members and friends will not be able to shoulder the burden alone.

The US Bureau of Labor Statistics (BLS) estimates the need for home health and personal care aides will increase substantially in coming years, requiring a 41 percent increase in the number of such aides needed by 2026.[51] Such aides generally have a high school diploma or the equivalent but don't undergo any extensive professional training prior to entering the health care workforce. Median pay is not very attractive either. In 2017, home health aides earned an average $23,210 annually, and personal care aides earned $23,100. In the Chicago metropolitan area, there are some 29,230 home health aides earning a mean hourly wage of $12.11.[52] Some 43,350 people were working as personal aides, earning a mean wage of $11.78 an hour.[53]

---

50 "2019 Alzheimer's Disease Facts and Figures," Alzheimer's Association, accessed July 10, 2019, https://www.alz.org/alzheimers-dementia/facts-figures.

51 "Home Health Aides and Personal Care Aides," *Occupational Outlook Handbook*, US Department of Labor, Bureau of Labor Statistics, accessed July 10, 2019, https://www.bls.gov/ooh/healthcare/home-health-aides-and-personal-care-aides.htm.

52 "Occupational Employment Statistics," US Department of Labor, Bureau of Labor Statistics, accessed July 10, 2019, https://www.bls.gov/oes/current/oes_16980.htm#31-0000.

53 "Occupational Employment and Wages, May 2017, Personal Care Aides," US Department of Labor, Bureau of Labor Statistics, accessed July 10, 2019, https://www.bls.gov/oes/current/oes399021.htm#st.

BLS also foresees increases in the number of registered nurses, licensed practical nurses, and certified nursing assistants. It estimates there will be a need for nearly 3.5 million registered nurses by 2026, an increase of 15 percent compared with 2016, which makes any form of licensed nursing an attractive career choice.

But not all the growth is because of aging baby boomers. Rather, it will occur in part because of the increased emphasis on preventive care and the growing rates of chronic conditions.[54]

RNs, who have at least a bachelor's degree, can expect to earn $36.84 an hour in the Chicago area, or $76,640 a year, higher than the national average. They coordinate patient care, help patients and the public understand various health conditions, and provide advice and emotional support to patients and their families.

Licensed practical nurses or licensed vocational nurses[55] also are expected to be in greater demand. Their number is expected to increase by 12 percent, or 88,900, by 2026.[56] LPNs and LVNs provide basic nursing care and work under the direction of RNs and doctors. Unlike RNs, though they need some postsecondary training, they don't need college degrees. In the Chicago area, they earn a mean hourly wage of $26.51, or $55,140 annually.[57]

CNAs generally receive on-the-job training and/or go through

---

54 "Registered Nurses," *Occupational Outlook Handbook*, US Department of Labor, Bureau of Labor Statistics, accessed July 10, 2019, https://www.bls.gov/ooh/health-care/registered-nurses.htm.

55 There is virtually no difference between an LPN and an LVN. They're called LVNs in California and Texas, but LPNs everywhere else.

56 "Licensed Practical and Licensed Vocational Nurses," *Occupational Outlook Handbook*, US Department of Labor, Bureau of Labor Statistics, accessed July 10, 2019, https://www.bls.gov/ooh/healthcare/licensed-practical-and-licensed-vocational-nurses.htm#tab-6.

57 "Licensed Practical and Licensed Vocational Nurses," *Occupational Outlook Handbook*, US Department of Labor, Bureau of Labor Statistics, accessed July 10, 2019, https://www.bls.gov/oes/current/oes292061.htm#st.

a state-approved program in order to qualify for a technical professional certificate. They then must pass a competency exam to become certified.[58] Their numbers are expected to increase 11 percent in the decade that began in 2016, when there were more than 1.5 million. There are some 39,770 nursing assistants in the Chicago area, earning a mean wage of $14.37, or $29,890 annually.[59]

THE FUTURE OF MEDICINE

Medicine has changed dramatically in the past two centuries, advancing at a pace few could have imagined. From the breakthroughs of microbiologists like Louis Pasteur in the nineteenth century to the gene-mapping and novel therapies of today, the goal always has been to improve community health and enable people to live longer, more satisfying lives. New drugs, advances in gaining control over immune systems gone awry, and technological solutions to paralysis promise hope to millions.

It's been a century since the Spanish flu wiped out as much as 5 percent of the earth's human population. There could have been a similar pandemic when the H1N1 virus started tearing around the globe in 2009, but the world was much better prepared. This time the death toll was 250,000 instead of millions. But that death toll still is too high. Getting a handle on just how bad an outbreak is takes too long because of the bureaucratic slowness involved in collecting data.[60]

---

58 "Nursing Assistants and Orderlies," *Occupational Outlook Handbook*, US Department of Labor, Bureau of Labor Statistics, accessed July 10, 2019, https://www.bls.gov/ooh/healthcare/nursing-assistants.htm#tab-1.

59 "Occupational Employment and Wages, May 2018, 31-1014 Nursing Assistants," *Occupational Outlook Handbook*, US Department of Labor, Bureau of Labor Statistics, accessed July 10, 2019, https://www.bls.gov/oes/current/oes311014.htm#st.

60 Michael Eisenstein, "Infection forecasts powered by big data," *Nature*, March 7, 2018, https://www.nature.com/articles/d41586-018-02473-5.

But what if researchers could use the internet to compile that data more swiftly? What if conventional monitoring could be married to streams of big data? Google came out with a flu-trend algorithm in 2008 that looked at user inquiries about flu symptoms and vaccine availability. It didn't work well in 2009, but it was a start. Since then, researchers have been able to map outbreaks of dengue fever and Zika virus, predicting where the outbreak would move next.

A move is afoot now to use smartphone apps to ask people directly about their health. Flu sufferers can report their symptoms on Flu Near You. In Europe, there's Influenzanet.

Electronic health records also could provide a vast resource for tracking disease, especially for those less common than influenza. But that leaves out countries that don't have such systems.

Antibiotics have done more in the last two centuries to improve survival rates than nearly anything else. But overuse of these miracle drugs has led to a crisis. Bacteria have adapted and become resistant, so we're running out of effective treatments. Though cutting back will help some, research for new drugs has been lacking, primarily because antibiotics don't bring in the big bucks for pharmaceutical firms that cancer treatments can produce.[61]

The prices for cancer-fighting drugs are staggering to doctors and patients, with some treatments exceeding an average $100,000 annually. The salaries of specialists and the costs of testing also are going up, as is radiotherapy and surgery. The trajectory is unsustainable and solutions are elusive. One suggestion is to pay for a drug only when it works. Call it an outcome-based price tag.[62]

There's no doubt developing life-saving drugs is expensive. Many

---

61 Natasha Gilbert, "Four Stories of Antibacterial Breakthroughs," *Nature*, March 7, 2018, https://www.nature.com/articles/d41586-018-02475-3.

62 "Bringing Down the Cost of Cancer Treatment, *Nature*, March 7, 2018, https://www.nature.com/articles/d41586-018-02483-3.

potential miracle drugs are languishing in research labs because there's no money to test them. One of the ideas to overcome this hurdle is to let the research drive the funding rather than the reverse, which is the way things are handled now. The suggestion is to treat the potential drugs as assets and create a megafund for 80 to 150, for which bonds would be issued to attract venture capital and money from other groups like pension funds.[63]

Despite all the disease-fighting progress that has been made, factors outside medicine are threatening to make once-believed vanquished diseases scourges in the future. Parents refusing to vaccinate their children, societal changes, and a host of other factors all threaten global health.[64]

And gene editing—known as CRISPR—is the most modern of new medical research techniques. It uses a synthetic RNA molecule and an enzyme from the bacterial immune system to change DNA. It can be used on genetic diseases as well as for drug discovery. The technique is precise. It can be used to turn genes on and off. We're talking unlimited gene manipulation.[65]

And mind reading isn't just for science fiction anymore—but we're not talking about divining what the person next to you is thinking. Rather it's the ability to transfer signals from the brain to a device that will allow the paralyzed to walk and those who have lost their ability to communicate with speech to think the words and project them on a screen. Scientists are working on brain implants that will stimulate damaged neural networks without putting so much

63 Roger Stein, "A bold new way to fund drug research," TED@StateStreet, accessed July 10, 2019, https://www.ted.com/talks/roger_stein_a_bold_new_way_to_fund_drug_research?referrer=playlist-the_future_of_medicine.

64 Hanna Barczyk, "The Future of Medicine 2018," *Scientific American*, May 16, 2018, https://www.scientificamerican.com/report/the-future-of-medicine-2018/.

65 Andrew Scott, "How CRISPR Is Transforming Drug Discovery," *Nature*, March 7, 2018, https://www.nature.com/articles/d41586-018-02477-1.

stress on the surrounding tissue that the tissue dies off.[66]

There are even more advancements in the offing: using 3-D printers to produce organs, eliminating the dearth of available organs for transplant; testing for Parkinson's disease with a phone call; using lasers to deliver drugs only to cells affected by HIV; using molecular markers to make tumors light up green, enabling surgeons to know exactly where to cut; more effective tools for detecting breast cancer; ultrasound surgery, eliminating the need to cut; needle-free vaccine patches.[67]

And if you thought, "How cool" when you first saw Bones use a tricorder on Star Trek, take heart. An emergency room doctor in Philadelphia has invented a working prototype of the handheld medical device that can scan a patient, read vital signs, and diagnose a problem in minutes. The device, the DxtER, is still awaiting regulatory approval. It looks like a medical kit with an orb-shaped digital stethoscope. It can measure lung function and take glucose readings, white blood cell counts, and perform other blood tests.[68]

The future is here.

---

66 "The Mind-Reading Devices That Can Free Paralysed Muscles," *Nature*, March 7, 2018, https://www.nature.com/articles/d41586-018-02478-0.

67 "The Future of Medicine," TED@StateStreet, accessed July 10, 2019, https://www. ted.com/playlists/23/the_future_of_medicine.

68 Sarah DiGiulio, "These ER Docs Invented a Real Star Trek Tricorder," *NBC News*, May 8, 2017, https://www.nbcnews.com/mach/technology/ these-er-docs-invented-real-star-trek-tricorder-n755631.

Conclusion

BrightStar Care of Central DuPage–Wheaton is more than a business. It's a way for us to give back to the community by providing a premium service that improves the overall health of the people who live in our area. Our services are necessary to enable those living in our service area in need of help live their best lives possible. As Michael Gerber says in The E Myth Revisited: Why Most Small Businesses Don't Work and What to Do about It, you can't force a business on a marketplace; rather, you have to fulfill a need. That's what we do: provide needed care to a population that wants our help in a way that is superior to any competitors.

> Anybody can provide care. We don't just provide it; we care about it.

We provide everything from basic caregiving a few hours a week to skilled-nursing care around the clock to staffing services at schools, doctors' offices, hospitals, and residential facilities. Our staff is well trained, dedicated, and attentive. As a client's needs change, we reassess and revise the care plan.

Anybody can provide care. We don't just provide it; we care about it. Caregiving is not a commodity to us. It's a product that evokes an emotional response. As Gerber puts it:

Ask anyone what kind of business they're in and they'll instinctively respond with the name of the commodity they sell. "We're in the computer business." Or, "We're in the hot tub business." Always the commodity … never the product.

What's the difference?

The commodity is the thing your customer actually walks out with in his hand.

The product is what your customer feels as he walks out of your business.

Understanding the difference between the two is what creating a great business is all about.[69]

> Unless a business asks its customers if they're actually getting the service they want, most businesses will never know.

We want our clients and their loved ones to feel good about the care we provide. Providing satisfaction—both to the client and ourselves—is key. There are a lot of options out there. Until we came along, those needing care sometimes had to accept less-than-optimal service. We have a culture that we have had from inception of meeting the client's needs and making sure the client is satisfied and the proper outcome is produced. We strive to be the best.

We learn what the needs of our clientele are and determine just

---

69 Michael E. Gerber, *The E Myth Revisited: Why Most Small Businesses Don't Work and What to Do about It* (New York: Harper Business, 1995), 153–54.

how we can meet them. Sometimes we have to say, "No, we cannot meet your needs." In that case, we say so and don't try to fake our way through a situation. Everybody says he or she provides a service, but unless a business asks its customers if they're actually getting the service they want, most businesses will never know. On our discharge paperwork, we ask if the patient goals and outcomes during the course of treatment were achieved.

Our nurse-case managers have a philosophy:

> A good conversation is essential to quality home care. Trust is built when someone feels understood and empathized with. This can be achieved by paying close attention and listening during a client conversation: You want to make sure that you relate to someone, and prevent relationship roadblocks.

> It is our belief that to relate to a client, a caregiver needs to feel engaged. Our nursing management team sees engagement as the key to equality—another condition for a successful relationship—and emphasizes that knowledge sharing with family caregivers strengthens it.

> Our BrightStar Care of Central DuPage–Wheaton caregivers are providing health assistance on your terms and your turf so your buy-in is mandatory to making it work.

I learned what good management is during my more than two decades at Testing Services Corporation, where they showed how much they valued their customers and employees.

We are not a home health agency. Home health is covered by

Medicare and is temporary. We are a private-pay home care agency, and there's no time limit on what we do or what we can do. If nursing services are required in addition to basic caregiving, one of our nurses can stop by and take care of the situation. If a caregiver requires a day off, we provide a substitute. Our clients never have to worry about a caregiver not showing up, unlike what may happen in private (nonagency) arrangements made through friends or the internet. Our clients get the undivided attention of their caregivers and nurses. There's no vying for attention as happens in assisted living or skilled-care facilities, where there are multiple patients to attend to.

COMMUNITY INVOLVEMENT

As longtime Wheaton residents, we care deeply about the community, donating time and money to causes that benefit such operations as Marianjoy Rehabilitation Hospital and the Northwestern Medicine Foundation.

My wife, Judy, started her nursing career at Central DuPage Hospital in 1968, and coincidentally I was involved in providing engineering services for multiple construction phases of that hospital system during my tenure at Testing Services Corporation. We have stayed close to the organization ever since. In addition to being active in the local business community, I took an interest in civic affairs, including stints as a township trustee. I want that involvement to continue after we're gone. As a result, it just seemed fitting for Judy and me to make a substantial estate bequest to the Northwestern Medicine Foundation, designed to advance the practice of home-based medical care in this community. The money we have committed is earmarked for HomeCare Physicians.[70]

---

70 "HomeCare at Northwestern Medicine Regional Medical Group," Northwestern Medicine Medical Group, accessed July 10, 2019, http://rmg.nm.org/what-we-offer/

"Central DuPage Hospital was the logical place to look to provide a gift," I told Northwestern Medicine's The Advisor's Bulletin in fall 2017.[71]

> Our health care mission at BrightStar Care focuses on caring for clients in their homes and is very similar to the mission of HomeCare Physicians," which has made more than 100,000 house calls since its inception in 1997.

> Judy and I have a deep respect for the work of everyone involved with HomeCare Physicians. They meet health care needs that, in some situations, would go unattended.

> We hope the gift will enable HomeCare Physicians to grow and widen its reach.

That wasn't our first donation. Our business has been donating annually to HomeCare Physicians for years—starting before we really could afford it. We've been recognized as a premier partner with the Northwestern Medicine Foundation, participating in their annual golf outing at Medinah Country Club—a favorite of the PGA—and the annual gala that benefits a variety of causes from pediatrics to geriatrics to cancer-patient support.

Clare Malysiak, director of philanthropy at Northwestern Memorial Hospital, said our involvement in these fund-raising efforts has helped support numerous initiatives, many of which can't be billed back to insurance companies, including the availability of

---

specialized-care/home-care?utm_campaign=Internal-RMG&utm_source=Vanity_link_print&utm_medium=homecare.

71 *The Advisor's Bulletin*, the Professional Council for Philanthropy, Northwestern Medicine, fall 2017.

social workers, art and music therapy, and many child life programs.

"They are wonderful, community-minded people and have always been very interested in giving back to the community in which they run their business. We are so very appreciative of that," Malysiak said.

OTHER INVOLVEMENT

BrightStar Care donates annually to ESSE, an area-wide adult day care service. We also partner with various fund-raising activities with Windsor Park Manor, a large retirement complex in our area, and we participate in memory walks and Parkinson's Foundation fund-raisers. In addition, we've partnered with the Chicago-area ALS Association, Les Turner ALS Foundation, and the American Cancer Society.

Though the vast majority of our referrals come from the North-western Medicine Central DuPage Hospital system, rehab centers, and medical professionals, we think it is important to make the community at large aware of our services and to educate them well enough so they know what questions to ask when it comes time to get help for themselves or a loved one. Many of those who make inquiries about care with us start with concerns about price, sometimes price only. From there, we need to convince people that issues such as licensing, medical expertise, Joint Commission accreditation, directly hired and trained employees, insurance, and bonding are matters that, yes, raise the price but are essential when seeking care for a precious loved one. Most care opportunities that come to us are in a time of crisis, and there is, of course, a certain amount of emotion involved. That's why client education is so important. It creates more common ground and less panic.

Small events at park districts, senior groups, the Wheaton Junior Woman's Club, the People's Resource Center, and DuPage Pads are the most effective ways of connecting with the public. We've also participated in Taste of Wheaton and held events at schools where we can engage with individual members of the audience and point them not only to our services but to other resources in the community (we provide a list of available services in the appendix to this book). We show how providing care is a collaborative effort among the client, the family, and our caregivers, CNAs, and nurses. No solution is perfect, but the more people are thinking and asking questions, the better it gets.

We recently held an ice cream social at ESSE and asked how many attendees were aware of BrightStar Care. Many said they were unaware of us and didn't know the difference between Medicare-paid home health and private-pay home care. They didn't know that Medicare only covers expenses up to a certain point, or that, like Medicare, long-term-care insurance pays only a portion of home care. This informal poll showed us there is still a lot of community-education opportunities for us to engage in!

People make better life choices when they're informed and aware of the help available. Not just health is involved. The home environment and the level of family resources available also must be considered. It lets us focus our energies where we can make the most impact. We break down the jargon that turns people off.

For example, assisted living is great until one member of a couple suddenly starts developing memory issues and the other needs rehab for a joint replacement or other medical issue. Suddenly, they can't live together in their unit any longer, and there's no guarantee their needs will get immediate attention, not when the CNAs are handling multiple patients and the nurses are overseeing two dozen at a time. In assisted living, one loses independence and autonomy.

Conversely, if that same couple had remained in their home, we could provide twenty-four-hour caregiving for the dementia patient while the spouse is in rehab and then reassess the needs once rehab is finished. Once home health has discharged the rehab patient, our caregiver can encourage the patient to keep up with his rehab exercises in addition to preparing meals and providing other services. Those services can be tailored to the couple's specific needs and wants, down to preparing favorite dishes for meals. You can't get that in assisted living. And the whole process is overseen by a registered nurse who is focused solely on the couple.

We cosponsor workshops on such issues as the latest techniques in dementia care or financial planning for insurance and long-term care twice a month for health professionals who need a certain number of continuing education hours to maintain their licenses.

ONE-ON-ONE

BrightStar Care is based on building trust and respect with patients and their families and providing personalized care solutions for an individual's medical conditions, lifestyle, interests, and environment. We do such one patient at a time. We demonstrate engagement with trusted referral sources, including primary care doctors, rehab centers, senior centers, hospitals, medical specialists, and family decision makers.

Gallup consistently has rated nursing as the most trusted profession by consumers. Trust is more than a feeling. It's a quality that can be measured in terms of patient satisfaction and impact on patient outcomes. To build trust, health systems must recognize the important role nurses play and ensure nurses are in positions to lead and influence efforts to create systems to promote the trust of patients and their families.

We do that. Our nursing team plays a vital role in coordinating prescribed home exercises, therapies, and activity restrictions. We are committed to keeping our clients as healthy as possible, and one of the ways to do that is to make sure they adhere to a medication regimen. Our nurses confirm prescription understanding, educate the family, monitor vital signs, follow up on side effects, ask questions about interactions with over-the-counter drugs, and report back observations to other medical professionals. All of these activities give an individual time to think about and recognize the effects of these medications on their overall health.

Providing quality care is more than a business to us. It is a mission, one that we long hope to fulfill.

Dupage County
Government Resources

Help is available throughout DuPage County through the county, state, and national organizations, delivering services ranging from meals to healthcare to legal matters:

- DuPage Senior Citizens Council, Lombard, 630-620-0804
- DuPage County Senior Services, Lombard, 630-620-0804
- DuPage County Community Information Resource System, Wheaton, 630-407-6500
- DuPage County Psychological Services, Wheaton, 630-682-7400
- Psychological Rehabilitation Program, Wheaton, 630-407-6400
- Access DuPage, Carol Stream, 630-510-8720
- Illinois Department on Aging, Chicago, 800-252-8966
- Illinois's Continuity of Care Association, estarman@franciscan-communities.com
- AIM-Center for Independent Living, Downers Grove, 630-469-2300
- Illinois Department of Veterans Affairs, Chicago, 312-814-2460[72]
- Metropolitan Family Services, Wheaton, 630-784-4800

---

72 "Pension," US Department of Veteran Affairs, accessed August 9, 2019, https://www.benefits.va.gov/PENSION/aid_attendance_housebound.asp.

- Senior Counseling, Chicago, 773-250-6202
- Prairie State Legal Services, Wheaton, 630-690-2130
- Respite Endowment Organization, Naperville, 630-204-0224
- Easter Seals DuPage & Fox Valley, Villa Park, 630-620-4433

DuPage Senior Citizens Council delivers meals to homebound seniors and is dedicated to helping seniors deal with daily challenges. The council does everything from well-being checks to minor home repairs to pet care. In addition to meals on wheels, the council also has dining centers set up throughout the county at which seniors gather to share a meal. The council helps seniors stay well informed on health issues, has volunteers who do yard cleanup, and provides contractor referrals for those who need more than minor home repairs. The council's friendly-visits program provides some companionship and intergenerational activities to help keep seniors connected to their community.[73]

DuPage County Senior Services offers a number of programs that help seniors remain independent after age sixty-seven. The services are funded through the Illinois Department on Aging and the Northeastern Illinois Agency on Aging.[74] The county has a case coordination unit, which publishes a senior-resource director, a long-term-care director, and a senior-housing directory. The county provides information to seniors, their families, and community agencies on accessing programs and services and offers in-home assessments to identify risks to independent living. The community care program

---

73   "Services" DuPage Senior Citizens Council, accessed August 9, 2019, https://www.dupageseniorcouncil.org/services/?gclid=EAIaIQobChMIqbH89vn73AIVibrACh2tk QT9EAAYAyAAEgI5-fD_BwE.

74   "Senior Services," The County of DuPage, accessed August 9, 2019, https://www.dupageco.org/seniorsvcs/.

provides homemaker and adult day services as well as emergency home-response systems. These services are provided free to those who qualify, while those in more secure financial positions can purchase the services. Case management follows up and monitors care plans, while the adult protective service handles abuse and neglect cases. The county has limited funding for residential repair and renovation. There's also a volunteer-based program to help with money management. The county will provide a consultant to help families decide on nursing and other facilities. A long-term-care ombudsman advocates for residents and investigates concerns and complaints. A community outreach program helps seniors who may be isolated because of transportation, housing, language, and other barriers. A federally funded family-caregiver support program provides information on respite services and emergency support. There's also limited funding for transportation for low-income seniors.[75]

DuPage County Community Information Resource System (DuPage CRIS) is a continuously updated database that provides the most current information on available resources. Among the information available is a list of free clinics.[76]

DuPage County Psychological Services is offered by the Health Department. Psychiatric rehabilitation helps individuals manage mental illness and build skills to allow them to integrate into normal community life and obtain prevocational training and residential

---

75 "Senior Services Programs," The County of DuPage, accessed August 9, 2019, https://www.dupageco.org/Community_Services/Senior_Services/1702/.

76 "DuPage Guide to Community Services," DuPage County CRIS, accessed August 9, 2019, http://dupagecris.org/index.php/component/cpx/?task=search.query&code=LN-1500.

services and enables them to achieve socialization and benefit from peer support.[77]

Psychological Rehabilitation Program partners with AMITA Health to offer immunizations, screenings, and health support to county residents.[78]

Access DuPage is a collaborative effort that provides access to medical service to county residents whose income is 200 percent below the poverty level and are ineligible for health insurance programs. Participating doctors try to provide a medical home for primary care services at nominal cost until individuals can obtain insurance. Enrollment is for a year, which can be extended on a case-by-case basis.[79]

Illinois Department on Aging advocates for older state residents and their caregivers. It administers programs that promote partnerships and encourages independence, dignity, and quality of life.[80] The department is funded through senior centers and other social service agencies. It has thirteen planning and service areas managed independently in partnership with twelve nonprofit corporations and the city of Chicago. DuPage County is handled by the Agency on Aging Northeastern Illinois,[81] which, like its associates, plans and coordinates services and programs for the elderly in the area. Funding

---

77 "Forensic Behavioral Health," DuPage County Health Department, accessed August 9, 2019, http://www.dupagehealth.org/Forensic-Services.

78 "AMITA Health Partnership," DuPage County Health Department, accessed August 9, 2019, http://www.dupagehealth.org/mental-health/resources/AMITApartnership.

79 Access DuPage, accessed August 9, 2019, https://accessdupage.org/.

80 Illinois Department on Aging, accessed August 9, 2019, https://www2.illinois.gov/aging/AboutUs/Pages/default.aspx.

81 Agency on Aging Northeastern Illinois, accessed August 9, 2019, http://www.ageguide.org.

is based on the number of older and minority residents in that area as well as the number living in poverty, in rural areas, and alone.

Illinois Continuity of Care Organization works to enhance the concept as an integral part of total patient care, advocating to the legislature and community about health concerns and issues. It also works with other organizations to support standards of professional competence.[82]

AIM-Center for Independent Living provides advocacy, independent-living-skills training, information and referrals, peer mentoring, and options counseling for the disabled.[83]

Illinois Department of Veterans Affairs works to help veterans and their families thrive, providing help with navigating the federal, state, and local services and benefits available, providing long-term health care for eligible veterans in veterans' homes, and working with other agencies and nonprofits in such areas as education, mental health, housing, and employment. The department is not part of the US Department of Veterans Affairs.[84]

Metropolitan Family Services provides patient and caregiver counseling and sets up evidence-based health promotional programs. The agency seeks to strengthen families providing help in education, job readiness, counseling, mental health services, and legal assistance.[85]

---

82   "2019-2020 Executive Board," Illinois Continuity of Care Association, accessed August 9, 2019, https://www.il-coc.org/board-of-directors.

83   AIM-CIL, accessed August 9, 2019, http://www.aim-cil.org.

84   Illinois Department of Veterans Affairs, accessed August 9, 2019, https://www2.illinois.gov/veterans/Pages/default.aspx.

85   "Programs and Services," Metropolitan Family Services, accessed August 9, 2019, https://www.metrofamily.org/programs-and-services/.

Senior Counseling Services helps physically, emotionally, and/or economically vulnerable older adults function as independently as possible. It includes in-home or office assessments, family and individual counseling, support groups, case management, and links to resources.[86]

Prairie State Legal Services provides assistance for older adults who need help with civil legal programs.[87]

Respite Endowment Organization supports families with special-needs children, special-needs adults with disabilities, and seniors. Its programs seek to relieve caregiver stress, depression, abuse, and neglect.[88]

Easterseals DuPage & Fox Valley raises funds for birth defect research and provides child screening, providing services for infants, children, and adults with disabilities as well as support for families. Its teams of therapists, teachers, and other health professionals help people overcome obstacles to independence and help them reach their goals.[89]

86 "Counseling," CJE, accessed August 9, 2019, https://www.cje.net/couns eling?gclid=Cj0KCQjw3KzdBRDWARIsAIJ8TMT4AHVrSozxcCg6tz5 iKG9_SCkuy4sViMRatUeAfVWmkYy4iP7WMLIaAvHGEALw_wcB.

87 Prairie State Legal Services, accessed August 9, 2019, https://www.pslegal.org/default.asp.

88 Little Friends, accessed August 9, 2019, http://www.respiteendowment.org/.

89 "Services and Programs," Easterseals DuPage and Fox Valley, accessed August 9, 2019, http://www.easterseals.com/dfv/our-programs/.

RETIREMENT AND ASSISTED LIVING

The best retirement communities in our service area include the following:

- Wyndemere Retirement Community, Wheaton, 630-690-6662
- Sunrise at Fountain Square, Lombard, 630-953-8990
- Windsor Park, Carol Stream, 877-770-4792
- Beacon Hill, Lombard, 630-620-5850

Wyndemere was established in 1993 and is dedicated to providing the best physical, emotional, and spiritual support possible. It is a life-plan community, meaning there's an up-front entrance fee that allows residents to move from independent living to assisted living, memory care, skilled nursing, and rehabilitation at no extra cost, except perhaps meals. Monthly fees are based on the size of the residence and the number of people living in it.[90]

Sunrise at Fountain Square offers assisted living, independent living, and memory care and is near Advocate Good Samaritan Hospital and Elmhurst Memorial Healthcare. The community has multiple patios, balconies, and gazebos for enjoying the outdoors. The chef prepares meals from scratch, and numerous activities programs are available. Sunrise is walking distance to numerous restaurants and near the Oak Brook and Yorktown shopping centers, Drury Lane Theater, and the AMC Yorktown movie theater.[91]

---

90   "Frequently Asked Questions," Wyndemere, accessed August 9, 2019, https://www.wyndemerelcs.com/about-retirement-community/faqs/.

91   Sunrise at Fountain Square, accessed August 9, 2019, https://www.sunriseseniorliving.com/communities/sunrise-at-fountain-square/.

Windsor Park is set up like a country club on sixty acres filled with trees, flowers, and lakes. Shopping, entertainment, and outdoor activities are nearby. Independent-living residents can choose among one-bedroom, two-bedroom, studio, and duplex apartments with private outdoor space and participate in scheduled activities or plan their own days. Educational opportunities also are available. When the time comes, residents can move into assisted living or skilled-nursing care.[92]

Beacon Hill Senior Living is a life-care facility with a median monthly rate for residents of $3,628.[93] Residents enter into a financial agreement for long-term-care services, paying an entrance fee and a monthly fee that does not increase significantly over time. It provides independent living, assisted living, memory care, long-term nursing care, and rehabilitation all in one place, allowing residents to age in familiar surroundings.

ASSISTED LIVING, TRANSITIONAL, AND MEMORY CARE

- Lombard Place Assisted Living, Lombard, 630-473-4079

Lombard Place Assisted Living is near both Advocate Good Samaritan Hospital and Elmhurst Memorial Healthcare. It boasts concierge services to help patients find a balance between independence and nursing assistance. Assistance is provided for daily living

---

activities. There's also an enrichment program, housekeeping services, and transportation.[94]

MEDICARE AND MEDICAID

- JourneyCare (home health, palliative, and hospice), Lombard, IL, 224-770-2489
- Addus HomeCare Inc., Downers Grove, IL, 630-296-3480

JourneyCare provides home health, palliative care, and hospice care for people of all ages living with advanced illness. As one of the largest community-based nonprofit hospice and palliative care providers in the Chicagoland area, JourneyCare continues to grow and expand to better serve its patients when and where it's needed most. JourneyCare just absorbed Northwestern Medicine Home Health & Hospice on April 22.

Addus offers home health services provided by nurses and physical, occupational, and speech therapists, as well as dietitians, medical social workers, and home health aides. These services can help avoid unnecessary hospitalizations, hasten hospital discharges, and enable an individual to remain at home during acute illnesses. These include Medicaid programs, veterans' benefits, other government programs, and long-term-care Insurance. Addus has reimbursement specialists who can handle the paperwork, ensure that individuals qualify, contact their payor to determine level of coverage, and then bill appropriately and directly on their behalf.

---

94 Lombard Place Assisted Living, accessed August 9, 2019, https://www.spectrumretirement.com/senior-living/il/lombard/lombard-place-assisted-living-and-memory-care/.

ACCOUNTABLE CARE ORGANIZATION FOR NORTHWESTERN MEDICINE + CMS (MEDICARE)

Cadence Health ACO LLC, d.b.a. Northwestern Medicine Physician Network ACO

1415 West 22nd St., Ste. 750E Oak Brook, IL 60523

Primary contact: Jessica Walradt, 312-926-5637, Jessica.walradt@nm.org

Helps consumers track Medicare Fee-for-Service beneficiary's services

ADULT DAY CARE

Adult day services provide a protective and stimulating environment for older adults in need of daytime supervision. It gives the attendee stimulation and caregivers a respite, in addition to a structured environment, meals, and a variety of activities. It's one way to mitigate the costs of in-home care. Schedules and fees vary, and financial assistance may be available through Veterans' Affairs or the Community Care Program.

- ESSE-Glen Ellyn Ecumenical Support Services for the Elderly, Faith Lutheran Church, Glen Ellyn, 630-858-1005
- ESSE-Wheaton Ecumenical Support Services for the Elderly, St. Paul Lutheran Church, Wheaton, 630-260-3773
- ESSE-Warrenville Ecumenical Support Services for the Elderly, Community Baptist Church, Warrenville, 630-791-9319
- Naperville Senior Center (serving the southern part of the county), 630-857-3017

ESSE provides stimulating experience for older adults with cognitive or physical problems. Nurses administer medication, perform monthly wellness checks, and develop care plans. Caregiver support is available weekly.[95]

Naperville Senior Center is open weekdays, 7:30 a.m. to 6:00 p.m., and staffed by nurses and physical therapists to help clients build or maintain strength, balance, and mobility. It serves adults with mild cognitive or physical disabilities.[96]

MEMORY CARE

Patients with Alzheimer's disease and other forms of dementia have special needs that require specialized care. Although some assisted living communities have memory-care units on premises, memory care is a distinct form of long-term skilled nursing that caters specifically to patients with various forms of dementia. Once patients reach the middle states of Alzheimer's, twenty-four-hour supervision is necessary for safety reasons. In choosing a facility, the level of family involvement should be assessed as well as the amount of medical and personal-care assistance provided. Examine the programs and services offered as well as the environment. Ask to see a weekly menu and examine the facility's policies and procedures. Costs vary depending on the facility and level of care needed, ranging as high as $97,455 a year. Costs are not covered by Medicare.

---

95   "Program Details," ESSE Adult Day Services, accessed August 9, 2019, http://www.esseadultdaycare.org/program-details.html.

96   Naperville Senior Center, accessed August 9, 2019, https://www.napervilleseniorcenter.com/senior-activity-center-naperville/.

- Arden Courts, Glen Ellyn, 630-469-5500
- Belmont Village Geneva Road, Carol Stream, 630-510-1515
- Brighton Gardens, South Wheaton, 630-681-1234

Arden Courts is staffed by specially trained caregivers who care for patients diagnosed with Alzheimer's disease and other forms of dementia. It features friendly common spaces, kitchen, and family rooms, along with walking paths with enclosed courtyards—all designed with the safety and comfort of residents in mind. The facility focuses on residents' capabilities and encourages maximum independence, with professional assistance available around the clock.[97]

Belmont Village Geneva Road is just down the road from Northwestern Medicine Central DuPage Hospital and downtown Wheaton. The community offers elegantly designed common areas and numerous menu choices at mealtime daily. Professional supervision is available at the fitness center, and free scheduled transportation is available. Residents live in studio and one-bedroom apartments, which are kept tidy by a housekeeping service. Belmont Village helps residents manage their medication and provides assistance with daily living activities. On-site rehab is available. There's no buy-in or long-term contract.[98]

---

97 Arden Courts, accessed August 9, 2019, https://www.arden-courts.com/locations/arden-courts-of-glen-ellyn/.

98 Belmont Village Senior Living, accessed August 9, 2019, https://www.belmontvillage.com/locations/geneva-road/.

Brighton Gardens of Wheaton, a Sunrise Senior Living facility, boasts a J. D. Power award for customer satisfaction in senior living. The staff encourages residents to engage, enjoy, express themselves, learn, and grow each day. They offer specialized Alzheimer's memory care and short-term stays at multiple levels of skilled assistance. Their managers develop personalized care programs geared to each resident's needs and preferences.[99]

BEHAVIORAL HEALTH

Behavioral health encompasses mental health as well as development and behavioral issues. These organizations offer evaluations and therapies for individuals to enable them to achieve the highest level of potential possible, overcome trauma, and conquer emotional problems and substance abuse.

- Northwestern Medicine Central DuPage Hospital, Winfield, 630-933-4234
- AMITA Health Behavioral Medicine Institute, Glendale Heights, 800-432-5005
- Linden Oaks Behavioral Medicine Outpatient Center, Naperville, 630-305-5027
- DuPage County Health Crisis Intervention Unit, Lombard, 630-627-1700

Northwestern Medicine offers a wide variety of support groups to meet specific needs. It coordinates inpatient and outpatient care for emotional and mental health issues, substance abuse, and addiction. Specialized services include treatment programs for teens, services for

99   "Brighton Gardens of Wheaton," Sunrise Senior Living, accessed August 9, 2019, https://www.sunriseseniorliving.com/communities/brighton-gardens-of-wheaton.

those facing both emotional issues and substance abuse, transcranial magnetic stimulation to treat severe depression, and psychiatric sub-specialties in addiction, geriatrics, and forensics.[100]

AMITA Health Behavioral Medicine Institute offers partial hospitalization, intensive outpatient treatment, and psychiatric and dual-diagnosis programs. Its multidisciplinary team of board-certified psychiatrists, clinical psychologists, addiction specialists, social workers, nurses, counselors, expressive therapists, dietitians, chaplains, and teachers coordinate with one another and medical specialists.[101]

Linden Oaks Behavioral Medicine Outpatient Center has a team of experienced psychiatrists, psychologists, physician assistants, advanced-practice psychiatric nurses, counselors, and therapists specializing in adolescent and adult behavioral health services. It has particular expertise in working with seniors.[102]

DuPage County Health Crisis Intervention Unit handles both emergency and nonemergency mental health services. The government agency provides professional counseling around the clock for emergencies. It accepts both Medicaid and Medicare as well as some private insurance.[103]

---

100 "Behavioral Health Services," Northwestern Medicine, accessed August 9, 2019, https://www.nm.org/conditions-and-care-areas/behavioral-health.

101 "Behavioral Medicine Institute," AMITA Health, accessed August 9, 2019, https://www.amitahealth.org/services/behavioral-medicine.

102 "Mental health services for seniors," Edward-Elmhurst Health, accessed August 9, 2019, https://www.eehealth.org/services/behavioral-health/specialties/mental-health-for-seniors/.

103 "Crisis Intervention Center," DuPage County Health Department, accessed August 9, 2019, http://www.dupagehealth.org/access-and-crisis-center.

SKILLED NURSING

Skilled-nursing care is provided for such things as complex wound dressings, rehabilitation, tube feedings, or rapidly changing health status. Medicare pays for at least sixty consecutive days of care, but that may be extended depending on the amount of progress being made, up to one hundred days per illness, with supplemental policies picking up coinsurance costs.

- Marianjoy Rehabilitation Hospital, Wheaton, 630-909-7000
- Wynscape Health & Rehabilitation at Wyndemere, Wheaton, 630-665-4330
- DuPage Care Center, Wheaton, 630-665-6400
- Lexington Health Network, Bloomingdale/Lombard, 630-495-4000/630-980-8700
- Johnson Health Care Center, Carol Stream, 630-510-5200

Marianjoy combines compassionate care with leading-edge technology. It has nationally recognized programs in stroke, brain injury, and pain management. Marianjoy participates in a number of research partnerships, providing patients with the most innovative therapies. More than forty-five thousand patients receive inpatient care, outpatient therapy, and doctor services annually for both acute and chronic conditions. It not only has Joint Commission accreditation; it is accredited by the Commission on Accreditation of Rehabilitation Facilities as well.[104]

Wynscape provides short-term rehabilitation services with the goal of returning patients to their homes after illness or hip, knee, or other

---

104 Marianjoy Rehabilitation Hospital, accessed August 9, 2019, https://www.marianjoy. org/.

joint-replacement surgery. Their physiatrists and nurse practitioners work closely with patients, their families, and their doctors to create an optimal outcome. Services include physical, occupational, speech, and orthopedic rehabilitation.[105]

The DuPage Care Center evolved from the County Alms House, built in 1888 for the area's indigent. It has developed into a modern, well-equipped, and professionally staffed treatment and rehabilitation center for the chronically ill. The center, providing both long- and short-term care, has 360 beds, 70 percent of which are dedicated to public-aid recipients and 25 percent of which are dedicated to those younger than fifty-five years of age.[106]

Lexington Health Network has a thirty-five-year record of providing health care and senior-living services. It provides skilled nursing care, therapy services, cardiac rehabilitation, pulmonary rehabilitation, orthopedic rehabilitation, and complex wound care. Lexington is privately owned, with more than 1,700 skilled nursing beds at ten postacute-, nursing-, and long-term-care buildings, in addition to 500 independent retirement units and more than 150 assisted living units in three senior-living centers.

The Johnson Health Care Center is part of Windsor Park, incorporating RehabAim to get patients back to their lifestyles as quickly as possible with efficient and effective rehab therapy. A staff psychiatrist manages rehab, bridging physical medicine, therapy, and pain

---

105 Wynscape Health & Rehabilitation at Wyndemere, accessed August 9, 2019, https://www.wyndemerelcs.com/health-services/senior-rehabilitation/.

106 "Care Center Overview," The County of DuPage, accessed August 9, 2019, https://www.dupageco.org/Convalescent_Center/6086/.

management. Patients receive customized one-on-one physical, occupational, and speech therapy seven days a week.[107]

HOSPICE AGENCIES

Hospice care is designed to provide support to people in the final phase of a terminal illness. It is focused on comfort and quality of life, not cure. The goal is to keep patients as comfortable as possible. Patients are eligible for hospice care if they are likely to live six months or less, but most people don't receive it until the final weeks or days of life. The care generally is provided at home, although there are some hospice facilities.

- Residential Home Health & Hospice, Downers Grove, 866-902-4000
- JourneyCare, Lombard, 224-770-2489
- Peace Hospice & Palliative Care, Naperville, 844-398-4459
- Seasons Hospice & Palliative Care of Illinois, Naperville, 800-570-8809

Residential Home Health & Hospice provides home health, palliative, and hospice services. Home health services include nursing and therapy while also providing support for care management and compliance. Its palliative services provide additional pain and symptom management for patients still seeking curative or rehabilitative treatments. Hospice care includes medical care, pain and symptom management, and support for end of life. The hospice team includes doctors certified in palliative care, nurse practitioners, social workers, and spiritual care counselors.[108]

---

107 Covenant Living at Windsor Park, accessed August 9, 2019, https://www.windsor-parkillinois.org/senior-rehabilitation-carol-stream-il.

108 "About Us," Residential Healthcare Group, accessed August 9, 2019, https://www.residentialhealthcaregroup.com/about-us/.

JourneyCare is dedicated to enriching the lives and providing compassionate care for hospice patients as well as those receiving palliative care. It is the largest nonprofit palliative care, support, and hospice provider in the state and serves nearly three thousand adults and children and their families daily. The goal is to care for the whole person, not just the disease, allowing those facing serious illness to live their lives to the fullest with dignity and without pain. Care is provided everywhere from home to hospital. JourneyCare also has five inpatient hospice facilities. The company was formed in 2015 through the merger of Horizon Hospice & Palliative Care, JourneyCare, and Midwest Palliative & Hospice Care Center.[109]

Peace Hospice, established a decade ago by Ronke Champion, provides dignified hospice care that upholds the self-respect and values of the individuals served. The agency provides assistance to patients and their families to improve quality of life for those with a terminal illness. The care team consists of the patient, family and close friends, the patient's doctor, and/or a hospice doctor, hospice nurse, hospice aide / homemaker, social worker, spiritual and bereavement counselors, and volunteers. Others who may be involved in the patient's care include a dietician; physical, speech, or occupational therapists; music therapist, and pharmacist.[110]

Seasons Hospice provides four levels of Medicare-certified care: routine, inpatient, respite, and continuous care. Its inpatient center provides a caring environment where patients get help for

---

109 "Expert Care Along the Journey," JourneyCare, accessed August 9, 2019, https://journeycare.org/expert-care-along-the-journey/.

110 Peace Hospice, accessed August 9, 2019, https://www.peacehospice.net/?gclid=Cj0KCQjw_vfcBRDJARIsAJafEnEN18Cm_ehJh9eLJop6qTvhfY5xBfD-KoLiR0--_BG8fRxU1BauyZHEaAgHsEALw_wcB.

the symptoms and loved ones can provide warmth and comfort.[111] Hospice professionals and trained volunteers work together to provide a holistic continuum of care around the clock as a patient's end of life draws near. For survivors, feelings of grief can be intense. Seasons offers bereavement support, including counseling, ecumenical and interfaith memorials, support groups, and written resources.

DOCTORS' OFFICES

Gerontology is a multidisciplinary medical field concerned with the physical, mental, and social aspects and implications of aging. Practitioners provide more specialized physical care and often work in nursing homes or hospices. Doctors who specialize in caring for the elderly are geriatricians, while a gerontologist generally has a nonmedical doctorate degree.

- Dr. Thomas Cornwell and Dr. Paul Chaing at Northwestern Medicine Regional Medical Group, Wheaton, 630-933-4800
- DuPage Medical Group, various locations, 888-693-6437
- Dr. Pauline Wiener, Carol Stream, 630-231-9400
- Dr. Anthony J. Pipitone, Wheaton, 630-653-0848
- Dr. James W. Scruggs, Wheaton, 630-510-6900
- Dr. Tessie Mathew, Carol Stream / Wheaton, 630-665-6500

HomeCare Physicians at Northwestern provides comprehensive medical care to homebound patients. The team is composed of primary care physicians and nurse practitioners who make house calls throughout the western suburbs, coordinating with hospitals, home health, and social service agencies. Services include blood testing, elec-

---

111 Seasons Hospice & Palliative Care, accessed August 9, 2019, https://www.seasons. org/about/locations/illinois/.

trocardiograms, gastrostomy tube changes, immunizations, in-home X-rays and ultrasounds, oximetry, tracheostomy tube changes, and wound care.[112]

DuPage Medical Group offers a full array of medical services to take care of the entire family, along with specialty services including geriatrics.[113]

Dr. Wiener is a psychiatrist affiliated with Northwestern Medicine Central DuPage Hospital, specializing in geriatric dementia.[114] Geriatric psychiatry focuses on dementia, depression, anxiety, sleep disorders, and late-life schizophrenia. Geriatric psychiatrists take a special approach to older adults who have special physical, emotional, and social needs and help families cope when issues arise.

Dr. Pipitone is an osteopath specializing in internal medicine. He is affiliated with Northwestern Medicine Regional Medical Group.[115]

Dr. Mathew is an osteopath specializing in geriatrics. She has special interests in women's health, palliative care, and preventive care.[116]

---

112 "HomeCare at Northwestern Medicine Regional Medical Group," Northwestern Medicine, accessed August 9, 2019, http://rmg.nm.org/what-we-offer/specialized-care/home-care?utm_campaign=Internal-RMG&utm_source=Vanity_link_print&utm_medium=homecare.

113 "Our Services," DuPage Medical Group, accessed August 9, 2019, https://www.dupagemedicalgroup.com/services/.

114 "Dr. Pauline Weiner," U.S. News & World Report, accessed August 9, 2019, https://health.usnews.com/doctors/pauline-wiener-18894.

115 "Anthony J. Pipitone, DO," Northwestern Medicine, accessed August 9, 2019, https://www.nm.org/doctors/1821010349?utm_source=yext&utm_medium=gmb%20physician&utm_campaign=online%20listings.

116 "Tessie Mathew, DO," DuPage Medical Group, accessed August 9, 2019, https://www.dupagemedicalgroup.com/our-physicians/tessie-mathew/.

PRIVATE MEDICAL TRANSPORTATION

- Angel Wheels Transportation, Naperville, 630-534-6900

Angel Wheels Transportation offers nonemergency transportation for the elderly, disabled, and their families. These services include medi-car and service car transport, attendant services to monitor health, private wheelchair access, and evening and weekend service hours.[117]

NONPROFIT COMMUNITY RESOURCES

Nonprofit organizations try to pick up where government resources leave off. DuPage County has a wide array of services available to help the needy:

- DuPagePads, Wheaton, 630-682-3846
- People's Resource Center of DuPage County, Wheaton, 630-682-5402
- Chicago Dental Society Foundation Dental Clinic, Wheaton, 630-260-8530
- College of DuPage Dental Hygiene Clinic, Glen Ellyn, 630-942-3250
- VNA Healthcare, Carol Stream, 630-892-4355
- Catholic Charities, Downers Grove, 800-941-8681
- Hamdard Center for Health and Human Services, Addison, 630-860-9122
- LivingWell Cancer Resource Center, Warrenville, 630-262-1111
- The Wellness House (for Living with Cancer), Hinsdale, 630-323-5150

---

117 Angel Wheels Transportation, accessed August 9, 2019, www.angelwheelsinc.com.

DuPagePads is dedicated to ending homelessness in the community, working to enable people to go from dependency to self-sufficiency. Founded in 1985, DuPagePads provides interim and permanent housing, coupled with support services like case management and life coaching, as well as employment support.[118]

People's Resource Center fights hunger with a food pantry. It also provides emergency rent and mortgage assistance; has "gently used" clothing for all ages; helps with emergency expenses; provides job assistance as well as computer-skills training, free computers, and computer repair; and offers tutoring for English, GED assistance, and help with citizenship exams. It also has services available to improve math and reading skills, as well as an art program.[119]

Chicago Dental Society Foundation Dental Clinic offers primary dental care at no cost to residents of Cook, Lake, and DuPage Counties.[120]

College of DuPage Dental Hygiene Clinic provides cleanings, X-rays, and bleaching for adults and children five years old and older. It has reduced fees but does not accept insurance.[121]

VNA Healthcare addresses the complex health needs of patients in their homes, linking mental and behavioral care with medical health

---

118 "About DuPagePads," DuPagePads, accessed August 9, 2019, https://dupagepads.org/about/.

119 "PRC Services," People's Resource Center, accessed August 9, 2019, http://www.peoplesrc.org/services.

120 "CDS Foundation Dental Clinic," Chicago Dental Society, accessed August 9, 2019, http://www.cds.org/clinic-details/cds-foundation-dental-clinic.

121 College of DuPage Dental Hygiene Clinic, accessed August 9, 2019, http://www.freedentalcare.us/li/college-of-dupage-dental-hygiene-clinic.

services. The organization does physical and mental health assessments. Its services include psychotherapy, cognitive therapy, stress management, addiction education, and grief resolution.[122]

Catholic Charities provides emergency assistance and homeless-prevention services to individuals and families in crisis. It also offers shelter, transitional housing, personal supportive housing, counseling, and adult day care.[123]

Hamdard Center serves community residents facing such challenges as the problems created by aging and domestic violence. It was founded on the idea patients receive the best care if their providers understand their cultural background and experiences. The staff speaks as many as ten languages.[124]

LivingWell Cancer Resource Center: The organization, operated by Northwestern Medicine, helps cancer patients and their caregivers learn the skills needed to regain control of their lives, reduce isolation, and enhance quality of life. Northwestern hopes to open a similar resource center in DuPage County.[125]

The Wellness House offers access to a variety of therapies, treatments, and techniques that can help cancer patients and families heal. Giving a voice to cancer struggles is important. Their programs and services are evidence based, facilitated by expert staff. They range from child

---

122 VNA Health Care, accessed August 9, 2019, www.vnahealth.com.

123 Catholic Charities—Diocese of Joliet, accessed August 9, 2019, www.cc-doj.org.

124 Hamdard Healthcare, accessed August 9, 2019, http://www.hamdardcenter.org/.

125 "Programs & Services," LivingWell, accessed August 9, 2019, https://livingwellcrc.org/programs-services/.

and family, exercise and nutrition, self-education, and stress management to support groups and counseling.

HOUSING AND UTILITIES

Several organizations help the homeless and work to keep people in their homes, including help in paying for utilities:

- Midwest Shelter for Homeless Veterans, Wheaton, 630-871-8387
- Senior Home Sharing, Naperville/Lombard, 630-407-0440, ext. 11
- HOPE House, Lombard, 800-941-8681
- H.O.M.E. DuPage, Wheaton, 630-260-2500
- Low Income Energy Assistance (LIHEAP), Downers Grove, 630-407-6500

Midwest Shelter for Homeless Veterans is dedicated to ending homelessness for veterans in northeastern Illinois and neighboring communities. The shelter was founded in 2000 by a Vietnam combat veteran who had been treating vets with posttraumatic stress disorder and a Desert Storm veteran. The first shelter opened in 2005 as a transitional housing program. In 2012 the group bought a building and converted it into six sober-living apartments for men and in 2015 opened a similar facility for women. It has programs for getting homeless veterans and their families off the streets and into permanent housing and job services, as well as a commissary where vets can purchase clothing and other supplies.[126]

---

126 "About," MSHV, accessed August 9, 2019, http://helpaveteran.org/about.

Senior Home Sharing has two residential buildings. House managers oversee activities and provide such services as meal preparation, light housekeeping, and medication reminders. Staff performs an assessment on new residents and works with them throughout their stay to make sure needs are met. They help seniors find such community services as depression screenings, quality-of-life screenings, health services, and social services.[127]

HOPE House provides temporary housing and support services to homeless individuals and families. It is run by Catholic Charities and has a twenty-four-hour crisis hotline.[128]

H.O.M.E. DuPage seeks to educate and empower individuals to be successful homeowners. Its emphasis is on serving first-time home buyers, low- and moderate-income households, and homeowners in crisis. The organization provides foreclosure, financial fitness, and reverse mortgage counseling. It also has an education program for first-time buyers.[129]

Low Income Home Energy Assistance Program (LIHEAP) helps offset energy costs and provides counseling, outreach, and education. Emergency assistance is available to eligible households in danger of disconnection or that already have been disconnected. It also will help homeowners in need of furnace repair.[130]

---

127 Senior Home Sharing, accessed August 9, 2019, www.seniorhomesharing.org.

128 "Catholic Charities – Hope House," DuPage County CRIS, accessed August 9, 2019, http://dupagecris.org/index.php/component/cpx/?task=resource.view&id=1313690.

129 HOME DuPage, Inc., accessed August 9, 2019, https://dhoc.org/.

130 "Low Income Home Energy Assistance Program (LIHEAP)," The County of DuPage, accessed August 9, 2019, https://www.dupageco.org/Community_Services/Client_Services/6068/.

DIAGNOSIS-SPECIFIC ORGANIZATIONS

The elderly are particularly vulnerable to diseases and conditions that manifest later in life. Numerous organizations work to educate the public on these ailments as well as raise money for research. These national organizations have offices in DuPage County or in Chicago:

- ALS Association, 312-932-0000
- American Cancer Society, 800-227-2345
- Alzheimer's Association, 800-272-3900
- American Diabetes Association of Illinois, 312-346-1805
- JDRF, 312-670-0313
- American Parkinson's Disease Association, 800-223-2732
- Illinois Arthritis Foundation, 800-735-0096
- Eldercare Locator Nationwide, 800-677-1116
- National Alliance for Mental Illness, 630-752-0066
- PACT Inc., 630-960-9700

ALS Association provides support for ALS sufferers and their families.[131]

American Cancer Society raises money for cancer research and provides educational materials.[132]

Alzheimer's Association provides referrals to local support groups, has online education materials, and raises money for research.[133]

---

131 ALS Association, accessed August 9, 2019, http://www.alsa.org/.

132 "American Cancer Society of Illinois," Facebook, accessed August 9, 2019, https://www.facebook.com/dupageacs.

133 "About," Alzheimer's Association, accessed August 9, 2019, https://www.alz.org/about.

American Diabetes Association of Illinois works to educate Illinois residents about the disease and support those afflicted with it. It also provides information to caregivers and others affected indirectly by the disease.[134]

JDRF raises awareness of juvenile diabetes and raises funds for research.[135]

American Parkinson's Disease Association provides resources for advocacy, health education, and respite. Its foundation works to improve care and advance research. Since 1961 it has raised more than $171 million for patient services and educational programs.[136]

Illinois Arthritis Foundation is focused on finding a cure for the disease and providing information, advocacy, science, and community.[137]

Eldercare Locator Nationwide helps match seniors with required services.[138]

National Alliance on Mental Illness is dedicated to providing support, advocacy, and education to improve the lives of those with mental illness and their families.[139]

---

134 "Illinois," American Diabetes Association, accessed August 9, 2019, http://www.diabetes.org/in-my-community/local-offices/chicago-illinois/.

135 "About JDRF," JDRF, accessed August 9, 2019, https://www.jdrf.org/about/.

136 "About APDA," American Parkinson Disease Association, accessed August 9, 2019, https://www.apdaparkinson.org/about-apda/.

137 "Illinois," Arthritis Foundation, accessed August 9, 2019, https://www.arthritis.org/illinois/.

138 Eldercare Locator, accessed August 9, 2019, https://eldercare.acl.gov/Public/Index.aspx.

139 NAMI of DuPage County, IL, accessed August 9, 2019, www.namidupage.org.

PACT Inc. provides case management of such things as identification, service planning, linkage, and advocacy for those with developmental disabilities, regardless of age.[140]

---

140 DayOne PACT, accessed August 9, 2019, www.pactinc.net.

Our Services

We cover a large section of DuPage County, including the communities of Wheaton, Bartlett, Bloomingdale, Carol Stream, Glen Ellyn, Glendale Heights, Winfield, and Lombard.

Our staff includes nonmedical caregivers, certified nursing assistants, licensed practical nurses, and registered nurses, all overseen by our director of nursing.

Home care: Basic caregiving is provided by nonmedical personnel; personal care is delivered by both nonmedical personnel and certified nursing assistants, including twenty-four-hour live-in care; and skilled-nursing care both for periodic tasks and twenty-four-hour nursing assignments is provided by licensed practical nurses and registered nurses. Our services include child care ranging from sitter services to skilled pediatric nursing, companion care to help support daily activities and monitor health and wellness, personal care for such tasks as bathing and grooming, senior care providing medication oversight and a comprehensive health assessment to keep seniors safe and active, transitional care to enable patients to return home after a hospital stay, home support and outside services to help seniors and other adults with everyday tasks, the ability to alter care should the need arise, and skilled-nursing care to attend to the most advanced medical needs.

Facilities staffing: We provide nurses and CNAs to hospitals, assisted living communities, skilled-nursing facilities, schools, hospice organizations, medical offices, therapy offices, adult day care centers, rehabilitation centers, home health care agencies, private-duty agencies, special-needs residential schools, on-site wellness and treatment clinics, flu-shot clinics, child-care centers, home infusion and dialysis services, workers' compensation providers and processors, and long-term-care-insurance providers and processors.

BRIGHTSTAR CARE OF CENTRAL DUPAGE-WHEATON

416 East Roosevelt Rd., Ste. 105
Wheaton, IL 60187
630-260-5300
https://www.brightstarcare.com/central-dupage-wheaton